The
Year
of the
Poet VII

September 2020

The Poetry Posse

inner child press, ltd.

The Poetry Posse 2020

Gail Weston Shazor

Shareef Abdur Rasheed

Teresa E. Gallion

hülya n. yılmaz

Kimberly Burnham

Tzemin Ition Tsai

Elizabeth Esguerra Castillo

Jackie Davis Allen

Joe Paire

Caroline 'Ceri' Nazareno

Ashok K. Bhargava

Alicja Maria Kuberska

Swapna Behera

Albert 'Infinite' Carrasco

Eliza Segiet

William S. Peters, Sr.

~ * ~

In order to maintain each poet's authentic voice, this volume has not undergone the scrutiny of editing. Please take time to indulge each contributor for their own creativity and aspirations to convey their uniqueness.

hülya n. yılmaz, Ph.D.
Director of Editing ~
Inner Child Press International

The Year of the Poet VII
September 2020 Edition

The Poetry Posse

1st Edition : 2020

Publisher Information

1st Edition : Inner Child Press
intouch@innerchildpress.com
www.innerchildpress.com

ISBN-13 : 978-1-952081-29-3 (inner child press, ltd.)

$ 12.99

WHAT WOULD LIFE BE WITHOUT A LITTLE POETRY?

Dedication

This Book is dedicated to

Humanity, Peace & Poetry

the Power of the Pen

can effectuate change!

&

The Poetry Posse

past, present & future

our Patrons and Readers

the Spirit of our Everlasting Muse

In the darkness of my life
I heard the music
I danced . . .
and the Light appeared
and I dance

Janet P. Caldwell

Table of Contents

The Poetry Posse

Table of Contents . . . *continued*

September's Featured Poets   113

Foreword

1990 Nobel Peace Prize recipient Mikhail Gorbachev the former president of Russia was the eighth and last leader of Russia's Soviet Union ' USSR. He held that office for about one and a half years early 1990 to August 1991. He held a number of high-level positions in a long active career as an organizer, activist, politician, statesmen etc. to list a few hats he wore. Note: His credits are massive so i will attempt to present an overview. He is noted for his progressive social/political leanings certainly by Soviet Russian standards a departure from the orthodox Communist party line.

Born in 1931 to a poor family of Russian / Ukrainian heritage. He grew up in the Joseph Stalin years and as a young man was involved in farming and operated combine harvesters on a collective farm. Combine harvesters are versatile farm machinery that harvest a variety of grain crops by performing reaping, threshing and winnowing thus combine harvesting. He joined the Communist party that governed the Soviet Union at that time as a one-party state under Stalin. At that time Gorbachev embraced the dominant, popular Marxist-Leninist doctrine. He entered Moscow State University where eventually met his future wife fellow student Raisa Titarenko. They married in 1953 prior to receiving his law degree in 1955.

He soon began working for a youth organization after Stalin's death became active in the ' de-Stalinization ' reforms of Stalin's successor Nikita Khrushchev. By this time, he was recognized enough to be appointed the First Party Secretary of the Stavropol Regional Committee in 1970. He continued to rise up in the party until he eventually became de facto head of government in 1985.

Around that time, it became apparent his social /political beliefs were beginning to develop a social/democratic slant in his thinking although still committed to preserving the socialist ideals of the Soviet state saw that it was time to engage in significant reforms especially after the 1986 Chernobyl disaster. Therefore, he withdrew from support of the Soviet-Afghan War, proceeded to establish dialog with United States President Reagan to limit nuclear weapons end the cold war. Domestically he introduced ' glasnost ' (openness) allowed for enhanced freedom of speech and the press. His 'perestroika' (restructuring) to improve economic efficiency, democratization measures, formation of the elected Congress of People's Deputies.

He declined military action when various eastern Bloc countries abandoned Marxist/Leninist governance in 1989-90 showing tolerance with their decision. Because of his untraditional governing an unsuccessful Coup attempt was made against Gorbachev in 1991. Afterwards the Soviet Union dissolved and Gorbachev resigned. He then launched his Gorbachev Foundation and he became a vocal critic against Boris Yeltsin and Vladimir Putin and campaigned for Russia's democratic movement. He became an advocate for the reunification of East and West Germany of course including bringing down the wall. He ultimately received the coveted Nobel Peace Prize in 1990 especially for his efforts to end the cold war.

Mikhail Gorbachev is an extraordinary human being with a record of amazing accomplishments over his life. He is a unifier bringing the world together in peace and harmony and he dedicated his life to that in a totalitarian regime that being Communist Soviet Russia, USSR and succeeded where others couldn't mainly because of his diplomatic skills and natural ability to connect with people across a broad spectrum of ideologies with dignity and respect affording dignity and respect to whoever he encountered. He is the consummate statesman and a major world figure of the second half of the 20th Century. Mikhail Gorbachev is a peacemaker!

Some of his significant accomplishments: Co-Chairman, Union of Social Democrats, second secretary, Communist Party of the Soviet Union, General Secretary Communist Party of the Soviet Union, Chairman Social Democratic Party of Russia, Chairman, Defense Council, Leader of the Soviet Union. Major player in the unification of

Germany, key contributor to end the Cold War which earned him the Nobel Peace Prize in 1990. Note: Remember this is just an overview.

Shareef Abdur-Rasheed,

International Author and Poet,
Cultural Ambassador
Inner Child Press International

Preface

Dear Family and Friends,

Yes I am excited and feel accomplished as we are on the last leg of our seventh year of publishing what I and many others deem to be a worthy enterprise, *The Year of the Poet*.

This year we have aligned our vision with that of Nober Peace Prize Recipients. We have title this year's theme. The Year of Peace! Hopefully thorugh our sharing each month, our poetry can have a profound effect on our global consciousness and the need for peace while educating ourselves and our readership about some of the individuals who have made history through their efforts to promulgate peace for all of humanity.. We are on our way to hitting yet another milestone. Needless to say, I am elated.

To reiterate, our initial vision was to just perform at this level for the year of 2014. Since that time we have had the blessed opportunity to include many other wonderful poets, word artists and storytellers in the Poetry Posse from lands, cultures and persuasions all over the world. We have featured hundreds of additional poets, thereby introducing their poetic offerings to our vast global audience.

In keeping with our effort and vision to expand the awareness of poets from all walks by making this offerings accessible, we at Inner Child Press International will continue to make every volume a FREE Download. The books are also available for purchase at the affordable cost of $7.00 per volume.

In the previous years, our monthly themes were Flowers, Birds, Gemstones, Trees and Past Cultures. This coming year we have elected to continue our focus of choosing what we consider a significant subject . . . PEACE! In each month's volume you will have the opportunity to not only read at least one poem themed by our Poetry Posse members about such celebrated Peace Ambassadors, but we have included a few words about each individual in our prologue. We hope you find the poetic offerings insightful as we use our poetic form to relay to you what we too have learned through our research in making our offering available to you, our readership.

In closing, we would like to thank you for being an integral part of our amazing journey.

Enjoy our amazing featured poets . . . they are amazing!

Building Cultural Bridges of Understanding . . .

Bless Up . . . From the home in our hearts to yours

Bill

The Poetry Posse
Inner Child Press Ineternational

PS

Do Not forget about the World Healing, World Peace Poetry effort.

Available here

www.worldhealingworldpeacepoetry.com

**For Free Downloads of Previous Issues of
The Year of the Poet**

www.innerchildpress.com/the-year-of-the-poet

World Healing World Peace
2020

Poets for Humanity

Now Available

www.innerchildpress.com/world-healing-world-peace-poetry

www.worldhealingworldpeacepoetry.com

www.worldhealingworldpeacefoundation.org

Mikhail Sergeyevich Gorbachev
1990

Each month for the year of 2020, which we have deemed as *The Year of Peace*, we at Inner Child Press International will be celebrating through our poetry a few Nobel Peace Prize Recipients who have contributed greatly to humanity via their particular avocations. This month of Julu 2020 you will find select poems from each Poetry Posse member on this month's celebrants.

In 1970, The Nobel Peace Prize was awarded to Mikhail Sergeyevich Gorbachev.

For more information about visit :

www.nobelprize.org/prizes/peace/1990/gorbachev/ biographical

https://en.wikipedia.org/wiki/Mikhail_Gorbachev

www.britannica.com/biography/Mikhail-Gorbachev

World Healing, World Peace Foundation
human beings for humanity

worldhealingworldpeacefoundation.org

xviii

Poets . . .
sowing seeds in the
Conscious Garden of Life,
that those who have yet to come
may enjoy the Flowers.

Poets, Writers . . . know that we are the enchanting magicians that nourishes the seeds of dreams and thoughts . . . it is our words that entice the hearts and minds of others to believe there is something grand about the possibilities that life has to offer and our words tease it forth into action . . . for you are the Poet, the Writer to whom the Gift of Words has been entrusted . . .

~ wsp

poetry is . . .

Poetry succeeds where instruction fails.

~ wsp

I FLY

because I can

...said the Dreamer to the world.

www.iamjustbill.com

Gail Weston Shazor

Gail Weston Shazor

This is a creative promise ~ my pen will speak to and for the world. Enamored with letters and respectful of their power, I have been writing for most of my life. A mother, daughter, sister and grandmother I give what I have been given, greatfilledly.

Author of . . .

"An Overstanding of an Imperfect Love"
&
Notes from the Blue Roof

Lies My Grandfathers Told Me

available at Inner Child Press.

www.facebook.com/gailwestonshazor
www.innerchildpress.com/gail-weston-shazor
navypoet1@gmail.com

Perestroika

Micky turned the tide
And the glass reflected
This nostic of knowing
Restructuring and
Reformation of the how
It was never about the what
For our Id of ology sustained
All that we have always been
One does not cease being
Adaptation moves everyone
Into the future
Whether we can see
On the other side
Or not
Sometimes a pane
Is only cleaned on the inside
For it is too far to
Fathom how far a drop
Exists on the outside
Glasnost

I want my poetry to…

I want my poetry to prepare you for death
Not for the grave
Nor the cemetery
But death
The end of all words
The end of all light
When you can sigh
And close your eyes in peace
Rested, relaxed
Sated
Satisfied that everyday
You healed yourself
From the trials of the day before

I want my poetry to prepare you for death
At the end of the conversation
Where thoughts meet pain
And pain meets joy
And joy is God
And God is good
Love conquers all, even the grave
I lower your body
Into the ground
And take your song
Into my soul four nourishment
Mind, spirit, breath and light

I want my poetry to prepare you for death
Starting this day
Let's not make a plan
To edify and rectify
Those that require one or both

Feed bellies and lay hands on brows
With a cooling touch
Set off fireworks in the streets
Just for pleasure of the blind
Let's do it

I want my poetry to prepare you for death
With words read
And colors painted
Threads running crookedly through a quilt
Linking, touching
The rough and smooth
Of moonlight
Broken glass prism-ed
Into beautiful satin
Music
Imagined in mentally challenged minds

I want my poetry to prepare you for death
The race run
And well set in clay
Steps to follow
A good example of a life fully lived
Under grace
Sometimes in sand
At the edge
Of tomorrow
But always looking
East
Prepared to follow the Son

Poets, I write about it

This Athenian hammer pounding against my skull
Begging to be birthed
In a slew of syllables and verbs
The unspoken anger
Of a child abused in their own bed
In their own home
In the keep of their own parents
Left unattended to the nightmares
That linger over into day
I will write
So that they know they are not alone
In this the circumstance of their birth
Not of their making
I will write the black eyes and pain
Hidden by pancakes applied
With a hot trowel against cheek and bone
The seams unravel across the skin of
Forehead and hip
Unexplainable damage that excuses
Were invented for
Raggedy edges where sense and purpose
Can't seem to meet
I will write
So they will know that it's ok
To leave in the dead of night
And steal back their souls
I will write the marks across
The backs of formerly strong black men
Of the young disenchanted men
That lead to the disenfranchisement of
A franchised prison system

That feed on the fears and legalities
Of the have not who must not
Because they are told not
And if you touch the fire, it is
More than a burning light
I will write
Of the shackled brains and concrete heads
Dropped off bridges feet first instead of
On open minds
I will write of open legs
Swathed in cotton, linen and gelatin
Painted green and only seen through
The lens of sunlit markers
Owed to the American dream
In heat and light and full bellies
Jobless, hopeless and hungry
Addicted to the street life
With no where else to go
I will write
So they are not forgotten and
Discarded as the unwanted, nameless
Bodies painted in pleasure
I will write those mournful tunes
Of elegies and dirges
Sung low in false basses of basements
A mother's baleful prayer
For the salvation of her kin
And the saving of her children
It cries to draw them back
From electric lights and intones
The dangers in drumbeats and howls
I will write the lyrics
Without notes and songs

Without the bars and stones
So we all can be free
I will write colors in the edges
So that those who live there
Will know that they are
More than in pieces
But pieces of the puzzle
And can be fit in the places
They were destined to be solid
Yearning for the peace of love
For the peace of life
I will write the lines
That draw them into this world
And separate them from that world
Built upon lies
I write

Alicja
Maria
Kuberska

.

Alicja Maria Kuberska – awarded Polish poetess, novelist, journalist, editor. She was born in 1960, in Świebodzin, Poland. She now lives in Inowrocław, Poland.

In 2011 she published her first volume of poems entitled: "The Glass Reality". Her second volume "Analysis of Feelings", was published in 2012. The third collection "Moments" was published in English in 2014, both in Poland and in the USA. In 2014, she also published the novel - "Virtual roses" and volume of poems "On the border of dream". Next year her volume entitled "Girl in the Mirror" was published in the UK and "Love me" , " (Not)my poem" in the USA. In 2015 she also edited anthology entitled "The Other Side of the Screen".

In 2016 she edited two volumes: "Taste of Love" (USA), "Thief of Dreams" (Poland) and international anthology entitled " Love is like Air" (USA). In 2017 she published volume entitled "View from the window" (Poland). She also edits series of anthologies entitled "Metaphor of Contemporary" (Poland)

Her poems have been published in numerous anthologies and magazines in Poland, the USA, the UK, Albania, Belgium, Chile, Spain, Israel, Canada, India, Italy, Uzbekistan, Czech Republic, South Korea and Australia. She was a featured poet of New Mirage Journal (USA) in the summer of 2011.

Alicja Kuberska is a member of the Polish Writers Associations in Warsaw, Poland and IWA Bogdani, Albania. She is also a member of directors' board of Soflay Literature Foundation.

A look to the future
A poem dedicated to Mikhail Gorbachev

Time crushes everything
It penetrates and attacks through
Powerful metal structures like rust
The strength begins to deteriorate
And the great powers are crumbling
like a bunch of cards

A few artifacts remain
Buildings are falling apart
And only the ground hides the foundations
Nations disappear
And immense empires
are only mentioned in textbooks

Captive peoples
Regain their former identity and boldly look up
History comes full circle
Slaves never stop
to dream about freedom

One has to be a visionary
To see the rules
governing the world and the future
He did not stick with the old one
When the wind of change
puts new boundaries on the world map

Do not burn the candles

Do not burn the candles
For me, my darling.
Do not call me.

I am the night butterfly.
I will fly to you,
Lured by warmth and flames.

My wings will burn
And I will stay forever
With you and your words

Request

Protect me,
Like a burning candle,
Against the gusts of life.

Take care of me.
I will give you warmth and light.
Build a raft of your fingers.
Do not allow me to sink
In the sadness.

I am imperfect
In this almost perfect world -
Ever more
Frail, faulty and weak

Jackie
Davis
Allen

Jackie Davis Allen

Jackie Davis Allen, otherwise known as Jacqueline D. Allen or Jackie Allen, grew up in the Cumberland Mountains of Appalachia. As the next eldest daughter of a coal miner father and a stay at home mother, she was the first in her family to attend and graduate from college. Her siblings, in their own right, are accomplished, though she is the only one, to date, that has discovered the gift of writing.

Graduating from Radford University, with a Bachelors of Science degree in Early Education, she taught in both public and private schools. For over a decade she taught private art classes to children both in her home and at a local Art and Framing Shop where she also sold her original soft sculptured Victorian dolls and original christening gowns.

She resides in northern Virginia with her husband, taking much needed get-aways to their mountain home near the Blue Ridge Mountains, a place that evokes memories of days spent growing up in the Appalachian Mountains.

A lover of hats, she has worn many. Following marriage to her college sweetheart, and as wife, mother, grandmother, teacher, tutor, artist, writer, poet and crafter, she is a lover of art and antiques, surrounding herself, always, with books, seeking to learn more.

In 2015 she authored *Looking for Rainbows, Poetry, Prose and Art*, and in 2017, *Dark Side of the Moon*. Both books of mostly narrative poetry were published by Inner Child Press and were edited by hulya n. yilmaz.

in 2019, No Illusions.Through the Looking Glass, which was nominated to be considered for a Pulitzer Prize by the publisher and editor of InnerChild Press, ltd.

http://www.innerchildpress.com/jackie-davis-allen.php
jackiedavisallen.com

Michail Gorbachev
Nobel Peace Prize Winner

As politician, he served the Soviet Union,
Both as president and Secretary General
Of the Communist Party,

And, today, looking back over his life
What memories holds he dear?
What awards, achievements earned?

What makes him most proud...his daughter?
The power he once wielded?
His pivotal role that ended the Cold War?

Or, a as reformer, his attempts
To turn the Soviet Union into
A socialist democracy?

In the darkness of sleepless nights,
Does he reflect back upon his political career?
With satisfaction? Despite notoriety's stains?

Blamed for the Soviet Reunion's demise,
Was resignation his only choice?
Do Russias's history books treat him well?

Clinging to his 1990 Nobel Peace Prize,
Does he savor the memory of planting seeds
That gave his countrymen people new rights:

The right to dream?
The right to think for themselves?
The right to manage their own lives?

Coming, As in the Morning

Down,
Deep down inside
Where the turbulence swirls

Self-talk indicts,
Shames.
Blames.

Alas,
Shadows of the past
Climb up and down the walls.

Silent,
The moonlight
Casts an eerie glow.

Gentle, like a summer breeze,
Mercy, peace, calm
And forgiveness

Comes in the morning
In response
To meditative prayer.

More Than Enough

Hands tied behind backs
And flags demeaned, accused
If ever lifted high, a salute
A traditional pledge deemed a crime

And silent prayers rejected
All in name of tolerance exacted
By those who say they are offended
Safe harbor, acceptance, comes

With responsibilities, with thanksgiving
Coming, accompanied with knowledge
Understanding, that there is no such thing
As an unencumbered free lunch

Nor does life comes as a trophy
In a goody bag
So, should not a nation remember
The words of one named Margaret

Yes, that's her name, she who once said
Something to the effect, the problem
With that kind of affair, is eventually

The state runs out of other people's money

Tzemin
Ition
Tsai

Dr. Tzemin Ition Tsai (蔡澤民博士) was born in Republic of China, in 1957. He holds a Ph.D. in Chemical Engineering and two Masters of Science in Applied Mathematics and Chemical Engineering. He is a professor at Asia University (Taiwan), editor of "Reading, Writing and Teaching" academic text. He also writes the long-term columns for Chinese Language Monthly in Taiwan.

He is a scholar with a wide range of expertise, while maintaining a common and positive interest in science, engineering and literature member. He is also an editor of "Reading, Writing and Teaching" academic text and a columnist for *'Chinese Language Monthly'* in Taiwan

He has won many national literary awards. His literary works have been anthologized and published in books, journals, and newspapers in more than 40 countries and have been translated into more than a dozen languages.

Perestroika

As ideology would never be doctrinal again
We are fighting for power
but only for power over people's minds

Those who look everywhere for internal enemies
Won't be a patriot
Comrades, you should not think about lifesavers but about
the ship

Between conflicting views
Accommodate greater openness and frankness
Oh, saw perestroika as encompassing a complex series of
reforms

A world without nuclear weapons
For mankind's survival
Political and religious freedom, the end of totalitarianism

See, all activities on Russian land have been suspended
Russian emperor tricolor empire flag
Waving on Staraya Red Square

What the devil knows
Just like a worn-out record
Silently spinning under the diamond tip of the worn
gramophone, resounding through the sky

The Soviet Union had ceased to exist
The Commonwealth of Independent States
Gladly accepted to be its successor, so far

Shadows

In a kingdom full of phantasms
And the changelings never overshadowing
The apparition smiled
I have dreamed of the treacheries
To warn me about the blur
I crave the soft, squint sunlight
Only this and a speciousness
Remembering many phantom, gnomish interstices
The fuzzier faerie fuzzing
And so you came gently baaing
The mists came withdrawing
Revoking and revoking with my pompousness
That hazy, hazy yanking
Back into my memories ceding
Long I stood there securing, speeding
Of the glowworm's that is succeeding
And its eyes have all the peeking
It was receding
I crave the backward, billowing breeziness
I crave the staring, sitting sky
Suddenly, I heard some glancing
And so I screamed, 'Is that a taciturnity?'

Apricot

In a kingdom full of storms
The storminess brought such sorrow
And the snowfalls never frosting
Only this and the almondy aintree aspiring
And its eyes have all the satisfying
It was trying
The twisters came blowdrying
The freesia seemed happy testifying
The convincing cloudburst craving
But in the fact that it was hissing
And the cladding was laving
The earthwork never craving
What could there be more purely raving?
Through which came looking
In there stepped a grilled shagbark hickory
The tanginess laughed
The delicious dijon drizzling
The thundery talking tiring
I crave the exhausting, enjoyable earthiness
The raspberry rosehip resurfacing
Enticing and enticing with my apricot tree
And so you came gently chattering
In there stepped a caraway grassiness
And the whirlwinds never flushing
All my soul within me rushing

Shareef
Abdur
Rasheed

Shareef Abdur-Rasheed, AKA Zakir Flo was born and raised in Brooklyn, New York. His education includes Brooklyn College, Suffolk County Community College and Makkah, Saudi Arabia. He is a Veteran of the Viet Nam era, where in 1969 he reverted to his now reverently embraced Islamic Faith. He is very active in the Islamic community and beyond with his teachings, activism and his humanity.

Shareef's spiritual expression comes through the persona of "Zakir Flo" . Zakir is Arabic for "To remind". Never silent, Shareef Abdur-Rasheed is always dropping science, love, consciousness and signs of the time in rhyme.

Shareef is the Patriarch of the Abdur-Rasheed Family with 9 Children (6 Sons and 3 Daughters) and 41 Grandchildren (24 Boys and 17 Girls).

For more information about Shareef, visit his personal FaceBook Page at :

https://www.facebook.com/shareef.abdurrasheed1
https://zakirflo.wordpress.com

Mikhail

----

ya Gorbachev
ya Mikhail
i want to say hail
but perhaps would
fail to avail Mikhail
his due
so, you think this is
a little strange
can't make of it
enough to maintain
the fact that this man
is extraordinary simple,
plain
yes, Gorbachev the name
a born leader
peace teacher
a born leader
peace preacher
a born leader
would've liked to meet ya
in the land of oppressive
suppression
or in another nation, venue
don't matter just meet you,
greet you and just listen
you wouldn't believe
free thinkers would become
leaders
and live to achieve things
beyond the status quo
and even receive respect
in a nation of repress

but Mikhail expressed
but Mikhail pressed
Mikhail tested the iron
fist
and brought hope to the
dance
where prior the band played
tunes about barbwire
from a hood called gulag
but even then, there were
those who dared to believe
all mankind received from god
the right to think, choose, refuse
Mikhail i respect you. Big-ups.
you're the man brother
though after you more
oppression of expression
continues to shackle many nations

food4thought = education

Multitudes..,

----

came ' n ' gone
back
where dem come from
every soul shall
taste of death
thy lord said
much blood
been spilled
soaked into ground
saturated rivers
fathers, mothers
sons, daughters,
grandmothers,
grandfathers,
sisters, brothers
long gone
like never born
we're here now
many deaf, dumb, blind
can't see, hear
except what they want to
be aware if it weren't for mercy
world and all it contains
would disappear in thin air
like it never was here
where's the god fear?
to recognize you wouldn't
breathe air if Allah*(swt)
didn't put it here
take a look around
survey earth sky to ground

even though many prayers
dem pray to whom they assume
hear their cries
but horrors continue
calamity, carnage on the menu
in plain view
served up, ^fitnah don't stop
many a prayer fall on deaf ear
praying to false deities
call dem taqut
bring darkness over you
misguided masses rely on lies
to get dem by
die in vain
like dem never came
praying in the wrong name

*(swt) = All glory to Allah.
^fitnah = mischief, upheaval,
disorder, mayhem

food4thought = education

reptiles..,
----
never crack a smile
as dem move fast
slither in the grass
no matter what disguise
dem take
a snake is a snake is a snake
like pitbulls folk get
dem say for protection
actually intimidation
there are human snakes
with guns 'n' badges
dem hide behind
proclaim
" serve ' n ' protect "
come down on poor
behinds
already in social,
economic binds
with evil intent
sent to
discourage, contain dissent
even though dem
sworn to serve, protect
instead there's
total disconnects
as far as human aspect
look at the faces
don't see themselves
as to those dem relate
where love, compassion equate
instead it's easy for them to

disrespect, feel hate
fueled by arrogance, ignorance
senseless bias dem accentuate
view that me and you something other
rather than sisters, brothers,
members of the human race
is there anything meaner that matches?
the demeanor of a cold blooded
snake?

food4thought = education

Kimberly Burnham

A brain health expert with a PhD in Integrative Medicine, Kimberly Burnham has lived in tropical Colombia; in Belgium during the Vietnam War; in Japan teaching businessmen English; in diverse international Toronto, Canada and several places in the US. Now, she's in Spokane, WA with her wife, Elizabeth, two sets of twins (age 11 & 14) and three dogs. Her recent book, *Awakenings: Peace Dictionary, Language and the Mind, a Daily Brain Health Program* includes the word for peace in hundreds of languages. Kim's poetry weaves through 70 volumes of *The Year of the Poet*, *Inspired by Gandhi*, *Women Building the World*, *A Woman's Place in the Dictionary*, Tiferet Journal, Human/Kind Journal and more.

https://www.nervewhisperer.solutions/
https://www.linkedin.com/in/kimberlyburnham/

Too Many Bombs and Bullets

Wonder what Mikhail would say today
thirty years after winning the Nobel Peace Prize
would he despair of another Russian diplomat
ever wining again
would he love the life of the Russian people
with 30 years of progress
would he be pleased with so many wars
burning hot
would he be happy with what the world has done
with his decisive contributions to peace

In 1990 when Mikhail Sergeyevich Gorbachev
won the Noble Peace Prize
the United States had 10,904 nuclear weapons
today there are 5,800
the Soviet Union had 37,000
Russia today has 6,375
12,175 ways to destroy our world

Albert Einstein said:
"bullets kill men,
atomic bombs kill cities
a tank is a defense against a bullet
there is no defense
against a weapon that can destroy civilization
our defense is law and order"

12175 While Even One

twelve thousand plus ways

the nuclear universe

all in madmen's hands

Mir Peace Word Heritage

We seem so different
but look at how much we have in common
most Slavic languages
"mir" means peace and quiet
Proto-Slavic is like the father
"mîrъ" both peace and world
Proto-Balto-Slavic's "meiˀrás" like the grandfather
and before that Proto-Indo-European's "meyH-ró-s" is
peace

Cousins show a resemblance Albanian "mirë" good
Latin "mītis" mild, calm and peaceful
Old Lithuanian "mieras" peace
Latvian miêrs peace, tranquility, calm, quiet and rest
as in "saglabāt mieru virs zemes" to preserve peace on earth

And a whole host of Slavic children
the East Slavic side of the family says peace
"мир mir mip myr"
Belarusian "mip" Ukrainian "myr"
Russian "мир" or "миръ" as in "мир во всём мíре"
"mir vo vsjóm míre" world peace
and universe, world, planet as in
"proisxoždénije míra" origin of the universe
where peace begins and in Russian Chuvash
"tănăş" and "мир" are peace
like Russian in Selkup "miř" means both
world and peace as does "mašar" in Chechen

And in Scandinavian Kildin Sami borrowed "мырр" or
"mɨrr"

the world and the peace from Russian pronounced uniquely
Skolt Saami "mēră" and Skolt Saami "mīr"
Akkala Saami "ḿer" and Ter Saami "mῑrr"

Peace in South Slavics' Old Church Slavonic is "mirŭ"
the same in Old Cyrillic "миръ" and Glagolitic "ⰿⰺⱃⱏ"
then Bulgarian, Macedonian, Croatian and Slovene
"мир" or "mir" as in "Мир и всичко добро!"
peace and all good
or Serbo-Croatian "центар града је оаза мира и зеленила"
city center is an oasis of peace and greenery

West Slavic siblings' Old Czech, Slovak, Carpatho-Rusyns
and
Old Polish "mir" or "mier" and Polish "ḿyr", "mńir" and
"mńyr"
all peace like Slovenščina's "ḿir"
Upper and Lower Sorbian's "měr"
while in Kashubian "mir" expands to true friend, peace,
quiet and stillness

Even lesser known languages like Erzya Mordvin say "mir"
Nanai and Gold use "Nomoȟon" and "mir" for peace
while in Kazakh "bejbetsilik", "mamır" and "мир" gives
peace
in Komi "miř" and "söglasön olöm" is peace
and in the Travellers' Macedonian Džambazi Romani
"Lačhipe" carries a whole host of meanings
goodness, good deed, benevolence, beauty, peace,
profit, well-being, fortune and
"mirno" is quietly, calmly and nicely

We can each find "mir" and a mirror
hold it up to the light
and in it see peace for all of us

Elizabeth E. Castillo

Elizabeth Esguerra Castillo is a multi-awarded and an Internationally-Published Contemporary Author/Poet and a Professional Writer / Creative Writer / Feature Writer / Journalist / Travel Writer from the Philippines. She has 2 published books, "Seasons of Emotions" (UK) and "Inner Reflections of the Muse", (USA). Elizabeth is also a co-author to more than 60 international anthologies in the USA, Canada, UK, Romania, India. She is a Contributing Editor of Inner Child Magazine, USA and an Advisory Board Member of Reflection Magazine, an international literary magazine. She is a member of the American Authors Association (AAA) and PEN International.

Web links:

Facebook Fan Page

https://free.facebook.com/ElizabethEsguerraCastillo

Google Plus

https://plus.google.com/u/0/+ElizabethCastillo

Gorbachev's Manifesto

Here was a noble man
Advocating for peace,
"The Marked Man" he was called
How can the world forget
His role in the Cold War?
Known for his glasnost
His policy of perestroika
That changed the face of Russia
He once said "If what you have done yesterday still looks
big to you,
You haven't done much today."

We Are Infinite

The Universe is vast
An ocean overflowing with mysteries
As we unravel each time
Even the darkest secrets of humanity.
As you look up the night sky
Full of stars, you start to wonder
Of your mortality, your One True Purpose
At times you might feel
Just like a small dot
Lost in oblivion
But do remember dear one
Even a speck of dust
Swirling in this endless madness
Remains part of of a whole.
Like a tiny pebble by the shoreline,
However small you are
You make a difference in this world.
As the beauteous constellations
Manifest in your naked eyes,
Illuminating the darkness
Like fireflies on a spree
In an enchanted forest,
Remember, we are infinite.
Our stories are borne out of one small story
And the cycle never ends
Like the circle of life
We are infinite
Our stories will have no ending
As we hold on to our dreams,
And we dare go follow our mystic flight
Discovering our predestined Personal Legend,
We are infinite.

Alabaster Dreams

They met amid The Plague
Twilight came
Dusk bade goodbye
Her sun-kissed cheeks
Illuminating the night sky
His alabaster skin
Shone in misty dew
Hands held
As they watch the stars
Unmindful of the world
Chasing dreams.

Joe
Paire

Joe Paire

Joseph L Paire' aka Joe DaVerbal Minddancer . . .
is a quiet man, born in a time where civil liberties
were a walk on thin ice. He's been a victim of his
own shyness often sidelined in his own quest for
love. He became the observer, charting life's path.
Taking note of the why, people do what they do. His
writings oft times strike a cord with the
dormant strings of the reader. His pen the rosined
bow drawn across the mind. He comes full-frontal
or in the subtlest way, always expressing in a way
that stimulate the senses.

www.facebook.com/joe.minddancer

Funny What You Don't Know

It's that time again, and time and time again
I'm faced with more knowledge
The old hammer and sickle were symbols of oppression
So many lessons of hiding under one's desk and
That never truly was going to work
We pride ourselves for sticking by ourselves
And borders are the enemy
People are the same despite the land they claim
So, we soldier up instead of friends to be
Here's the epiphany for me you see

This man behind the "Iron Curtain"
This cold war that we feared
earned the noble peace prize
and an actor got the cheers
Mikhail Sergeyevich Gorbachev was no actor
He had a thing for education
and war? War was not his agenda,
although We tend to think so, and democracy
Was not about the amount of goods sold
Truly a misquote but the gist is this

He cared for his people, kind of reap what you sew
Change from the top down was the way to go
It's strange that we talk now about letting democracy go
"if not me who? If not now? When"
Yes, indeed I'm quoting again
Us versus them, clashes between borders
Religion against religion social disorder
Is there a win for democracy? Or a spin to democracy?
For those who tinker with polices think again
It's funny what you don't know

Boom, Splash, Bang, Meow

I'm on that onomatopoeia tip now
Maybe I'm referencing my inner stooge
The first time I heard of this word
I was educated by three fools
Poetic definitions in my time of stress
I rhyme for less, but I'm under duress
Crash upon my window, like the snare of rain
Tinkle like those keys of piano fame
Smash like Hulk, or a super mutant
Buzz was like the sound of a bee
Now rumor has it, the buzz is about me

Onomatopoeia describes the sound I read, hear?
a little grapple with an apple, hiss come here dear
Pow, Zap, Bonk, honk, Bow wow or arf-arf
Please don't forget woof-woof
Or the sound that's made when bacon's cook
Sizzle isn't it? Lean, not so much
But a click clack means her heels are stacked
As she echoes down my corridor
Like the flutter of a raven's wing,
Long live poor Elenore

Whoosh, wham, bam thank you ma'am
What connotations are these, onomatopoeia
Or the confessions of a sleaze?
The crackle of a fireplace's hearth
Or cereal with the addition of snap and pop
We hear these words and know the meaning
Feeling, tasting, even smells can be revealed
The sound of peace is not silent
And silent words can make you feel.

Packing Up and Moving

I can't say there is no love lost because it is
I'm surrounding in boxes packed for another tier
My mother's tears fall dry
My father's years go by, and I'm stuck in limbo
The fast and curious moved me into this reality
How can one sort and fold their abnormalities
I leave behind remnants of me, my soul tends to linger

Foreclosed to a better singer but I write the songs
Daring to share, not caring if there are complications
I suck at communication, now I'm forced to commute
Same me in a different space, that does not compute
I left a roadmap to my crap, that is not in dispute
Labeled and tabled a misfit,
being true to one's self is hard to admit
now I must admit I didn't put in the work
I wasn't fit to be something other than my quirk.

Empty drawers and dressers, boxes full of letters
Tape that doesn't want to stick
And the kids, God bless them, won't do
Well you know, another room packed to go
Renew this, renew that, reconnect my services
To the new space I'm at, man I hate moving
It's been loves demise, as I add to my list of dismissals
Still I rise packing up and moving.

hülya
n.
yılmaz

Liberal Arts Emerita, hülya n. yılmaz is a published author, literary translator, and Co-Chair and Director of Editing Services at Inner Child Press International. Her poetic work appeared in an excess of eighty-five anthologies of global endeavors and has been presented at numerous national and international poetry events. In 2018, the Writer's International Network of British Colombia, Canada honored yılmaz with a literary award. As of 2017, two of her poems remain permanently installed in *Telepoem Booth* – a U.S.-wide poetic art exhibition. hülya finds it vital for everyone to understand a deeper sense of self, and writes creatively to attain a comprehensive awareness for and development of our humanity.

Writing Web Site
https://hulyanyilmaz.com/

Editing Web Site
https://hulyasfreelancing.com

disillusioned . . .

you must have faced a savage opposition
fanaticism ran deep also in your beloved country
your 1990 Nobel Prize for peace speaks for itself
you have overcome obstacles during your presidency

i often wonder these days
if your birth into the life of regular people
– not *with a silver spoon in your mouth,*
as we say here in the good ol' US of A,
was what molded into the essence of you
your non-exclusive dedication to humanity,
to your people's wellbeing and sanity

the entire world is now under the threat of a deadly virus
some countries' leaders have taken – ever so swiftly –
effective measures to control its wide-reaching spread
among their populace – affectionately, all-inclusively –
everyone in every nation today needs such leadership direly
yet several self-serving holders of a seat of high command
go about their own business while they continue to demand
that we bow down, keep silent, and accept what is at risk,
not persist with our questioning
and not insist on our rights
which we are too close to losing
with a hastened move of the leading hand's swing

oh, how welcomed would be to have a peace icon like you
if only we could rise above these dark times – all intact –
as if reaching to touch a sky of hues in azure blue

disillusioned?
oh, yes, i am,
about the good i believed that was all-embracingly true

A Renga for Gorbachev

My dear poet-friends:
Your collaboration is needed on this one.
Here is my stanza . . .

you worked for democracy
Communism, destroyed
Fascism is in

A HAIKU for Democracy

politics is flawed

tried and failed regimes galore

democracy rules!

Teresa E. Gallion

Teresa E. Gallion was born in Shreveport, Louisiana and moved to Illinois at the age of 15. She completed her undergraduate training at the University of Illinois Chicago and received her master's degree in Psychology from Bowling Green State University in Ohio. She retired from New Mexico state government in 2012.

She moved to New Mexico in 1987. While writing sporadically for many years, in 1998 she started reading her work in the local Albuquerque poetry community. She has been a featured reader at local coffee houses, bookstores, art galleries, museums, libraries, Outpost Performance Space, the Route 66 Festival in 2001 and the State of Oklahoma's Poetry Festival in Cheyenne, Oklahoma in 2004. She occasionally hosts an open mic.

Teresa's work is published in numerous Journals and anthologies. She has two CDs: *On the Wings of the Wind* and *Poems from Chasing Light*. She has published three books: *Walking Sacred Ground, Contemplation in the High Desert* and *Chasing Light*.

Chasing Light was a finalist in the 2013 New Mexico/Arizona Book Awards.

The surreal high desert landscape and her personal spiritual journey influence the writing of this Albuquerque poet. When she is not writing, she is committed to hiking the enchanted landscapes of New Mexico. You may preview her work at

http://bit.ly/1aIVPNq or *http://bit.ly/13IMLGh*

From Poverty to Nobel Prize

Gorbachev was born in poverty.
Moved from Marxist to communist
to socialist principles over the
course of his life. Served in
many political capacities and continued
to grow, evolve, change and adapt
to different ideologies.

He believed significant reform
was necessary. He withdrew from
Soviet Afghan war, attended summits
to limit nuclear weapons
and end the Cold War.

It is saying it mildly to state he lived a life
of political controversy while at the same time
effecting change.

He continues to be a controversial figure
who won the Nobel Peace Prize
for his role in ending the Cold War,
curtailing human rights abuses
in the Soviet Union and tolerating both
the fall of Marxist-Leninist
and the reunification of Germany.

Intimate Hold

I have intimate moments
sitting by the river.
The clouds get jealous,
turn gray and threatening.
The river still distracts
with loving caresses.

I look up at the clouds
as they hold back tears.
What stories of suffering
do they shelter as the thunder
growls in measured tones.

I want to move,
give the clouds space.
The river won't let me go.

Climbing into Ecstasy

She wandered through
the colonies of physical love,
tested the branches of desire.
None held her up.
Her soul cowered in a fetal sadness
she tried to ignore.

Today she finds herself
in the presence of the Beloved
who touches her forefinger.
Her soul steps out of the fetal curl,
moves toward the approaching light.
Her body tries to resist
but the pull of love beyond the physical
is impossible to reject.

The first time her heart
feels the pull of love,
she surrenders.
Her soul floats in love's light
climbing into ecstasy.

Ashok
K.
Bhargava

Ashok Bhargava is a poet, writer, community activist, public speaker, management consultant and a keen photographer. Based in Vancouver, he has published several collections of his poems: Riding the Tide, Mirror of Dreams, A Kernel of Truth, Skipping Stones, Half Open Door and Lost in the Morning Calm. His poetry has been published in various literary magazines and anthologies.

Ashok is a Poet Laureate and poet ambassador to Japan, Korea and India. He is founder of WIN: Writers International Network Canada. Its main objective is to inspire, encourage, promote and recognize writers of diverse genres, artists and community leaders. He has received many accolades including Nehru Humanitarian Award for his leadership of Writers International Network Canada, Poets without Borders Peace Award for his journeys across the globe to celebrate peace and to create alliances with poets, and Kalidasa Award for creative writings.

Perestroika: Restructuring

Not even the rising sun could
lighten up the dark secrets.

Amnesia shrouded hierarchy concealed
beneath corruption and cruelty.

Helpless citizens like caged
wingless birds craved for the sky.

Gorbachev realized
there was a need to repair

the wrinkled Soviet system
imposed from above

without any input from
grassroots.

Décor of Kremlin was peeling
off with tears of pain.

With the fervor of a revolution he initiated
perestroika to restore dead dreams.

He could not withstand the forces
of change himself.

Glasnost: Openness

I like to sing a song
for the old and young
to stir cravings
for their lovers.

Not for the clashing of tanks
for bloodshed nor for conflict
but songs to thrill the hearts
longing for life.

I like to sing for openness
for peace and harmony.

I like to sing
for humanity
for they are
the radiance
bloom
spirit
smile
and the meaning of my words.

Departure

I tear
the heart of the mountains
at the speed of a shooting star.
I trample
the canyon roads from
Kamloops to Banff, in search of
a bindi placed on
her forehead carefully
trying to incarnate.
Karma will probably not allow it.

At night
all stars allude to be same.
I wonder if perestroika has disarrayed
the red star over Moscow or the star over
the Tiananmen Square
is dimmer now or
the blue star of David has reincarnated
on the Golan Heights like
a bindi on her forehead?
I can't be sure about the nationality of stars.

Like winding roads entwine
the mighty Rocky Mountains, her arms
around my neck and her soft body
hard pressed against mine,
wrings my soul
with a force of an avalanche.
A vagrant tear on the edge of her eyes,
twinkles like a star.
A goodbye in its most subtle form,
a time of departure for me.
Beneath the starless sky,
I don't know my destination.

Caroline
'Ceri Naz'
Nazareno
Gabis

Caroline 'Ceri Naz' Nazareno-Gabis, World Poetry Canada International Director to Philippines is known as a 'poet of peace and friendship', a multi-awarded poet, editor, journalist, speaker, linguist, educator, peace and women's advocate. She believes that learning other's language and culture is a doorway to wisdom.

Among her poetic belts include 7 th Prize Winner in the 19 th and 20 th Italian Award of Literary Festival; Writers International Network-Canada ''Amazing Poet 2015'', The Frang Bardhi Literary Prize 2014 (Albania), the sair-gazeteci or Poet Journalist Award 2014 (Tuzla, Istanbul, Turkey) and World Poetry Empowered Poet 2013 (Vancouver, Canada). She's a featured member of Association of Women's Rights and Development (AWID), The Poetry Posse, Galaktika Poetike, Asia Pacific Writers and Translators (APWT), Axlepino and Anacbanua.

Her poetry and children's stories have been featured in different anthologies and magazines worldwide.

Links to her works:

panitikan.ph/2018/03/30/caroline-nazareno-gabis
apwriters.org/author/ceri_naz
www.aveviajera.org/nacionesunidasdelasletras/id1181
.html

Timeless Words of Gorbachev

"If not me, who? And if not now, when?"
Those words remind my worth
To embrace my hometown
Just like you did
You become the grassroot
Of freedom and openness.

"If not me, who? And if not now, when?"
Those words are tender
Which gives probe of your firm leadership
Your enthusiasm and youthful energy
Sparked positive change,
There was hope in your hands.

"If not me, who? And if not now, when?"
Those words are galvanized
To build a community
Which developed a strong relationship
You have restructured the Soviet
And the Berlin Wall…
You are the boulder
The maker of Peace.

Thank You, My Child
For Yali

There was a sudden rupture
which gave me an agonizing
pain on the eleventh hour; it became a miracle,
I become an empowered woman. I am now a mother.

I called God and the angels to be with me as
I signed the most sacrificial experience
to give birth to our little sun,
who would bring extra warmth and sunshine into our lives.

I celebrate life because you are life.
I can see the vivid radiance on your toothless smiles,
 mysterious coos and grunts, and unexpected cries while
you're asleep.

Your father was in tears,
when he knew, you and I were both safe,
and saw you at 4:30 on the 23rd of Martian June.

Our lives are even brighter now, as a family.

Why You Are Born

my little darling, my daughter,
one day, you would become
the bravest soul,
transformed like the butterfly,
days may come and go
as you live through changes ...
you 'll bloom with dreams and miracles,
once, twice or many times
you'll wither,
but remember, you are born
to make a difference...
so don't stop believing
in your dreams.

Swapna Behera

Swapna Behera is a bilingual contemporary poet, author, translator and editor from Odisha, India. She was a teacher from 1984 to 2015. Her stories, poems and articles are widely published in National and International journals, and ezines, and are translated into different national and International languages. She has penned six books. She is the recipient of the Prestigious International Mother Language UGADI AWARD WINNER 2019. She was conferred upon the Prestigious International Poesis Award of Honor at the 2nd Bharat Award for Literature as Jury in 2015, The Enchanting Muse Award in India World Poetree Festival 2017, World Icon of Peace Award in 2017, and the Pentasi B World Fellow Poet in 2017. She is the recipient of Gold Cross of Wisdom Award, the Prolific Poetess Award, The Life time Achievement Award, The Best Planner Award, The Sahitya Shiromani Award, ATAL BIHARI BAJPAYEE AWARD 2018, Ambassador De Literature Award 2018, Global Literature Guardian Award, International Life Time Achievement Award and the Master of Creative Impulse Award. She has received the Honoured Poet of India from the Seychelles Government accredited Literary Society LLSF. Her one poem A NIGHT IN THE REFUGEE CAMP is translated into 50 languages. She is the Ambassador of Humanity by Hafrikan Prince Art World Africa 2018 and an official member of World Nation's Writers Union, Kazakhstan 2018. Italy, the National President for India by Hispanomundial Union of Writers (UHE), Peru, the administrator of several poetic groups, and the Cultural Ambassador for India and south Asia of Inner Child Press U.S.

in a profound solitude

in a profound solitude
the sun rises in its zenith
mystery of love and Sufi melody
march forward in the carnival
I listen the waves of commanding words
the spasmodic time creeps
my heart counts the centuries
game starts
winners become the losers
and the victory is celebrated
the roads wait for the grand celebration
the clarity behind the masks
pour thunder for rains
portals and domains open the door
almost every moment rises inside me
a vacuum reflects myriads of exhilarations
new portraits are hung
a climax gives the clarion call
the river joins the sea
I become we........

tea shop

here is the teashop
in the narrow street
of this city
groups of people taking morning tea
a news paper lying on the bench
as a pregnant woman ready to deliver
dozens of glasses active ;
discussion starts
before the election

the last night event
murder or theft
clumsy shop becomes crowd
the shop serves information informal
parties or politics free of cost

daughter's marriage
 death of a neighbour
house on sale or rent
life as it goes on

a tea shop
the life line of a city
 a young lover or old granny
the strong and the tall
a student or professors
a tea shop gathers

a tea shop
gives solution
the first line of a poem

the climax of a novel
a torrential storm
a horse latitude
a husband's last solace
after a domestic dispute

a tea shop in the city
a committee of gaiety ....

the hero who ends the cold war

he was the Soviet president
but resigned
the post was abolished
the Russian federation flag raised
the last leader of the Soviet Union
ends the cold war

he was the planner of glasnost and perestroika
glasnost to increase openness, transparency
a commitment to allow the citizens of soviet union
to discuss publicly the problems and potential solution

 perestroika for complete restructuring the economy
that allowed local managers
to elect their own representatives
more authority over the farms and factories
to own small business
 taking care of macroeconomy
including price control

his new thinking was to shut down
 the costly cold war competition ;
 reform the economy through expansion
the Berlin war came down in Germany

"Peace is not the unity in similarity but unity in diversity"
he is Mikhael Sergeyevich Gorbachev
the noble peace prize laureate
history remembers forever.....

Swapna Behera

Albert 'Infinite' Carrasco

Albert 'Infinite' Carassco

Albert "Infinite The Poet" Carrasco is an urban poet, mentor and public speaker.

Albert believes his experience of growing up in poverty, dealing with drugs and witnessing murder over and over were lessons learnt, in order to gain knowledge to teach. Albert's harsh reality and honesty is a powerfully packed punch delivered through rhyme. Infinite grew up in the east part of the Bronx and still resides there, so he knows many young men will follow the same dark path he followed looking for change. The life of crime should never be an option to being poor but it is, very often.

Infinite poetry @lulu.com

Alcarrasco2 on YouTube

Infinite the poet on reverbnation

Infinite Poetry

http://www.lulu.com/us/en/shop/al-infinite-carrasco/infinite-poetry/paperback/product-21040240.html

Mikhail Gorbachev

Mikhail Gorbachev was born on March 2 1931 in
Privolnoye Russia,
He was raised by a poor family,
In his youth he worked on a farm before joining the
communist party.
While studying in Moscow State he married a fellow
student named Raisa,
Later on they would have a child, a daughter, Irina.
Mikhail Gorbachev became a Russian and former Soviet
politician.
The eighth and last leader of the Soviet Union.
He was the president from until March 15 to August 19
1991.
Mikhail Gorbachev acknowledged for many achievements
and received many awards.
He won the Nobel Peace Prize by peacefully ending the
Cold War.
When it comes to peaceful solutions, he never gave up,
His acts led to a chain reaction which led to the fall of
communism in Europe.

No future plans

I didn't really plan for the future growing up in the slums because growing up in my hood we die young. It was about the here and now, living for the moment pushing white girl trying to turn a project building into a cash cow. We weren't dumb poverty had us naive to the soul thieves.

Hunger is a blinder, by any means we was making sure that there was breakfast, lunch and dinner. In that past there was no guarantee for neither of three. We all had dreams of becoming breadwinners, we became sinners, bidders and work for gravediggers.

Some had bands on top of bands and never spent it remembering fucked up dealt hand, some splurged daily because during our oppression we dreamt to be in a position where we can blow a few grand at any given time on materialism.

Shopping sprees turn into addiction, you get side tracked by wants and lose focus on needs, the only thing that worked as trick'n rehabilitation was coke recessions, when you're down to your last "one's" you realize that you have to do better with bloody income.

There was a lot of forgotten sons living in darkness hoping to see the sun, I saw the start and finish of many runs, not many got to retire, most expired, ya know, freezer, glued eyes, lips and last three days on earth attire.

Casualties of war, casualties of raw, it's as if an entire generation is under dirt or behind bars and walls. To the survivors from that era... blessings to you all.

My Genre

I lived my poetic genre so my pen will never run dry. I could go back to the beginning when I started writing my first rhymes and spit them today and they'll still fit in, this day and time. Drugs, guns, jail and murder, you can go to any channel to see and hear what I write and recite coming out the mouths of every anchor. History is on repeat. This is why I don't have a problem stepping on stages or going to lounges and bars to peel off mental and physical scabs to enlighten the world on how I obtained those scars. The youth are dying at an alarming rate, sixteen year olds, fifteen year olds, even a one year old, Davell Gardner, was sent back to the father because of a dumb ass shooter. Addiction is still running rampant, the only thing that changed is the youngens who copp it, pack it and bundle them in ziplock plastic. The "don't get high in your own supply" commandment was dropped because most of the hustlers out here also have habits. "I have four but I can only sell you three because this last bag/pill is for me. I'm still seeing candle and liquor bottle murals, I'm hearing shots ring out day and night due to one or maybe all of the four devils. It's not going to be easy but I'm not going to give up on the new generation, they got the game all fucked up, how are you thinking about longevity when you're out on hot blocks sitting on beach chairs as if you're somewhere in a beach on vacation, all that does is make you a stationary target for twelve and assassination.

Eliza Segiet

Eliza Segiet - A graduate of Jagiellonian University, The author of poetry volumes. *Romans z sobą* [*Romance with Oneself*] (2013), *Myślne miraże* [*Mental Mirages*](2014), *Chmurność* [*Cloudiness*] (2016), *Magnetyczni* (2018) *Magnetic People*- translation published in The USA in 2018, *Nieparzyści* [*Unpaired*] (2019), A monodrama *Prześwity* [*Clearance*] (2015), a farce *Tandem* [*Tandem*] (2017), Mini novel *Bezgłośni* [*Voiceless*](2019). Her poems can be found in numerous anthologies both in Poland and abroad. She is a member of The Association of Polish Writers and The World Nations Writers Union. The laureate of The International Annual Publication of 2017 for the poem Questions, and for the Sea of Mist in Spillwords Press in 2018. For her volume of Magnetic People she won a literary award of a Golden Rose named after Jaroslaw Zielinski (Poland 2019 r.). Her poem The *Sea of Mists* was chosen as one of the best amidst the hundred best poems of 2018 by International Poetry Press Publication Canada. In The 2019 Poet's Yearbook, as the author of *Sea of Mists*, she was awarded with the prestigious Elite Writer's Status Award as one of the best poets of 2019 (July 2019).

She was awarded *World Poetic Star Award* by World Nations Writers Union – the world's largest Writers' Union from Kazakhstan (August 2019).

In September 2019 she was 1st Place Laureate (Foreign Poetry category) – in Contest *Quando È la Vita ad Invitare* for poem *Be Yourself* (Italy).

Her poem *Order* from volume *Unpaired* was selected as one of the 100 best poems of 2019 in International Poetry Press Publications (Canada).

In November 2019 she is a nominee for Pushcart Prize.

Restructuring
To Mikhail Sergeyevich Gorbachev –
Nobel Peace Prize Laureate 1990

Peace

it's crossing barriers

–from coexistence to collaboration,

it's unity in diversification, not in symmetry.

Secure, peaceful future

created thanks to *perestroika*

–through chance, to win without wars,

because lack of violence

-is a base of peace

Translated by Ula de B

Experiences

Everywhere we will be
the past will be with us.
We cannot escape from it –
it has always been and will be
a part of ourselves.

We will not erase the imaginations
that –
in confrontation with reality –
may seem even strange.

And our experiences
will be
– sometimes silence,
– sometimes screaming,
they can be an oblivion
when the mind says
enough.

Translated by Artur Komoter

Pause

When asked about the staff of life,
she could not explain.

It's simple:
birth,
childhood,
youth,
old age
and inevitable death.

It also happens otherwise,
one cannot add up to five.

Cruel time
has set a pause on the future.

Translated by Artur Komoter

William S. Peters Sr.

Bill's writing career spans a period of over 50 years. Being first Published in 1972, Bill has since went on to Author in excess of 50 additional Volumes of Poetry, Short Stories, etc., expressing his thoughts on matters of the Heart, Spirit, Consciousness and Humanity. His primary focus is that of Love, Peace and Understanding!

Bill says . . .

I have always likened Life to that of a Garden. So, for me, Life is simply about the Seeds we Sow and Nourish. All things we "Think and Do", will "Be" Cause and eventually manifest itself to being an "Effect" within our own personal "Existences" and "Experiences" . . . whether it be Fruit, Flowers, Weeds or Barren Landscapes! Bill highly regards the Fruits of his Labor and wishes that everyone would thus go on to plant "Lovely" Seeds on "Good Ground" in their own Gardens of Life!

to connect with Bill, he is all things Inner Child

www.iaminnerchild.com

Personal Web Site

www.iamjustbill.com

I apologize

We have painted your country,
Your people
As a focal point,
Of our ugliness,
Our ignorance
And our enemy

I apologize to you,
And the people
For my dark perceptions
About things
I do not,
Did not
Know

Over 16 million lost
Fighting a war,
By our side
That you could have avoided
It you were willing to acquiesce
To the fascist values
Of the German Machine
Of human dastardly-ness . .
But you did not

And along come you Sir
Mikhail Sergeyevich Gorbachev,
Championing the rights
Of the people,
Not only that of your beloved Russia,
But that of an entire world

I thank you
For your great contributions
To democracy.
I apologize
For my ignorance

I embrace your humanity

Lost

We have walked through these fields
Of self-delusion
Much too long . . .
Are we lost, yet again?

I remember times
Such as these
When we sailed the
Uncharted seas
Of consciousness
Seeking adventure
Looking at times
For safe harbour
During the storms . . .
We survived,
Did we not

I often ask the questions
How & Why

Perhaps our purpose
Is just that ! . . .

They say,
It is what it is !

.....

Perhaps we are but wanderers,
Travelers,
Wonderers,
Seeking something
We thought misplaced

Funny isn't it,
And here we are not
Going the way
We once prescribed,
Prophesied,
The way of the ancients ?
……..

Upon a path
Of no end,
A road with no juncture
Where we must decide
The Greater or the 'Lessor'

Yes there are hills,
Here and there,
But the mountains
Have all but disappeared
As we have come upon this new
Seemingly,
Never-ending plateau
Where there is a faint horizon
Beyond the beyond

There is no East
Nor West,
No North,
Nor South . . . .
But I maintain
My point of personal reference
For I do sense still
An Up
And a Down
And most importantly

That which is 'Without'
About me
And that which is 'Within' . . .
Whispering in
A coded language
Without refrain
Over and over again
……
Oh these damned conundrums
…..

This gives me hope
Within this forced solitude
Where the platitudes
Grow upon me
Without cease . . .
Oh, where is my peace,
Where is my peace
……
And then there is silence

Time now

Close thine eyes
And hold to
Your inner self,
And let go of
All that you see,
And all that you think you see

Let your senses become rejuvenated
Enlivened
And smell,
Feel,
Hear,
Taste
The essence of change
That is about to consume us

The prophecies of old
Told of these days
To come,
And they now are here
Banging loudly
Violently
Upon the doors
Of ignorance
That have stood guard
To our delusional consciousness
And ill-guarded hearts

By the wagon-loads,
Cart-load,
Bus-load,
Plane and Train-loads

People are dying
In the midst of their personal vying
For a better life . . .

Perhaps they found
They received
That temporary reprieve
They conceived
They deserved . . .

We are being served
Poisonous meals
Of diffusion
Divisiveness,
Deceit
And delusion,
And we eat,
We eat,
We eat,
Consuming the instruments
Of our own demise

But, a few
Shall rise
Above the fray . . .
Maybe not today,
But soon
A way will be revealed,
And the abyss-way to hell
Will be sealed . . .
Forever
Until the next
TIME . . . NOW

September

2020

Featured Poets

~ * ~

Raed Anis Al-Jishi

Šolkotović Snežana

Dr. Brajesh Kumar Gupta

Umid Najjari

i Fly

because I Can

... said the Dreamer to the world.

Raed
Anis
Al-Jishi

Raed Anis Al-JISHI is a poet, translator Qateef -; Saudi Arabia. He has an honorary fellowship in writing from Iowa university-USA . A member of advisory committee of exquisite Teacher training plan of national Changua University of Education-Taiwan . has translated 5 books. And published one novel, nine volumes of poems in Arabic(last one was translated into French) and one Bleeding Gull: Look, Feel, Fly, in English(this book was translated into Serbian,Vietnamese and Italian languages and win the best translated book in Italy in tow deferent occasion . A lot of his single poems were translated to many languages.

The Arrival of Seagulls

I have seen gulls,
in holy visions,
hover and invent
the sound of horses.

I have seen them
give alms to rats
hungry for crumbs of bread,
crucified on the altar.

I have seen them
flap their wings and swallow
common rules of fish.
Reinvent the physics
of a silver talisman's dance
on the sea's curve.

I have seen rats
feast at the fall of dusk.
They claim to be the genesis of light.
….

Final Act

In the theatre of time I stand crucified on the cross of my
tongue
watching birds as they fall on my song

And steal breadcrumbs and wine
that grow from my soulful melody.

What could meaning hide for me
if the bars of its rhythms are rooted in the rhyme's soul?

I see nails pierce through my hands,
and yet my dreams hammer back.

I am a stranger carving out the meaning of home,
recollected from memories my footsteps have known.

This home that lends its marks on my skin
and prints thorns on branches of my veins.

A cooing carved, while clouds witness
the towering dance in my lungs.

Water escaped the land to pour upon me
and drench the cracks of my murmur.

Some words can't grow without a body
unless slain in the temple of description.

What if I didn't listen to my heart?
My cross is all I carry with me

This heart I bear on my back bent
serene with my songs into the woods.

My verse metrics sound the storm in my blood
against this world of dust that dulls the spirit.

I hear string echoes calling for the uprising
within the confines of my time and space.

I'm a free soul, and my soul tortures me,
likely to stitch my lips into silence.

Yet my word will take me among
the scented stream of flowers gilding my guillotine.

Only poems soothe my wanderlust
in one poised moment.

Two raptors surround me: my mind & my faith.
A whispering angel with broken wings

Walked seven times around my remains
ringing my hums in every round.

I will break the pink stone inside my chest
if she leaves me in a valley with no direction.

And I will cut the oxygen of love,
if she tries to break my illusions.

…

A Dance of Bullets

If out of passion I strained my heart,
it doesn't matter.
You crossed each alley
of my inner streets -
mirrored the dream
running through my veins,
and from my garden,
plucked,
the love grown
from a pear tree.

If I offer you roses
distilled from my blood
and if, in your honor
I play the anthem of salvation
with my heart's beats,
it doesn't matter.

Home,
it doesn't matter.
It doesn't matter if
all you could offer me is
a dance of bullets.

Šolkotović
Snežana

Šolkotović Snežana

Šolkotović Snežana is a supervisory teacher in elementary school. Writing is her hobby. She has published poems and stories for children and adults in fourteen books: Song is my Life, From a Heart to Heart, In the Name of Love - Cruel fate, The Source of Life, When the Soul Speaks, The Whisper of the Wind, The Children's Jest, Doohickey, Dodge; a Serbian-English bilingual collection The Horizons of Love; a Serbian-Italian bilingual collection The Call of the Hearthstone / IL RICHIAMO DEL FOCOLARE and The Dawn Of Life - L'ALBA DELLA VITA; a Russian-Serbian collection of poems The Soul's Poetry. Some of her poems are translated into Bulgarian, English, Arabic and Macedonian language. Many of her poems and stories are featured in numerous anthologies, collections and journals. She has won prestigious awards at domestic and international competitions.

Biografija:

Šolkotović Snežana profesor je razredne nastave. Pisanje joj je hobi. Objavila je pesme i priče za decu i odrasle u četrnaest knjiga:- Pesma je moj život, Od srca srcu, U znaku ljubavi-Surove sudbine, Izvor života, Kad progovori duša, Šapat vetra, Dečja zavrzlama, Zvrčka, Smicalice, dvojezičnoj zbirci, srpsko- engleska, Horizonti ljubavi Horizons of love, zastupljena je i u dvojezičnoj srpsko-italijanskoj zbirci Zov ognjišta/ IL RICHIAMO DEL FOCOLARE i Zora života - L'ALBA DELLA VITA, rusinsko- srpskoj zbirci pesama Poezija duše- POEZIЯ DUŠI. Neke od njenih pesama prevođene su na bugarskom, engleskom, arapskom i makedonskom jeziku. Mnoštvo pesama i priča zastupljeno joj je u mnogobrojnim antologijama, zbornicima i časopisima. Osvojila je prestižne nagrade na domaćim i međunarodnim konkursima.

For A Happy Childhood

It takes a little to have a happy childhood,
Great love of the parents,
A place under the blue sky…
A consolation hug, the impulse to fulfill your desires,
An ear for the secrets and support from friends.

A special story which only grandma knows,
A grandfather's quip and a joke while solving a problem…
A fireplace warmth that selflessly comforts the soul,
A pet and the family in whole.

Children's happiness is like a butterfly,
And a family is a place where you can enjoy
and dream the most...
It takes a little to have a happy childhood,
And that little would fit into two words only.

"I love you." - pleases everyone equally,
Hugs and tenderness is what everybody crave,
Parental love means a lot to a child,
With support and security,
One becomes safer and stronger ...

Let's Save Our Planet

Let's save our planet,
A bright future for every child,
Where they could grow happily,
To keep an eye on the swallow's flight,
To walk on earth fearless,
With optimism and no threats.

Let's keep our planet safe,
It is the only home of the whole world,
Where beautiful gardens are streched,
Dreams come true like fantasy spells.

Let's save our planet,
A butterfly's flight to a colorful flower,
A blue vault and water deep,
Flowery meadows; fragrant.

Let's keep our planet safe,
Since there is no other for us,
It represents life for all people,
Let's keep it as the air that is inhaled,
Because of everything that lives here,
and much more...

Let's save our planet,
Thus we will save ourselves, too.
Without it - other values are worthless.
Let's protect our planet,
The future of humanity; the world.
Everyone is equally entitled to it,
To keep it alive and call it a "mother".

Just A Kid

To the children,
The world is marvelous,
A lot can be done there,
A smile is enough,
A hand provided,
Sadness in the eye without saying a word is seen.

Everything is beautiful in its own way,
Life has its own charm,
It can understand us all,
And forgive a lie.

In this world,
Happiness reigns,
The flower lures the sleeping bee,
Each petal is dear to it,
And the clown in a funny suit.

Magical are the words of love,
That gently crash the mistakes,
And the mere expanse of a child's soul.

The world of the child is wonderful,
It can be complex,
And interesting in its own way every day,
A priceless contribution to this is the children's fate.

Only a child can enjoy that world,
Makes it beautiful by its presence,
Because the magic of this world is imagination,
And an inexhaustible genuine love.

ZA SREĆNO Detinjstvo

Za srećno detinjstvo samo malo treba
velika ljubav roditelja,
 mesto ispod plavog neba…
Zagrljaj utehe, podstrek za ostvarivanje želja
uvo za tajne, podrška prijatelja.
Ona posebna priča koju zna samo baka
dosetka i šala dede, prilikom rešavanja zadatka…
Toplina ognjišta koja duši nesebično prija,
kućni ljubimac i cela familija.
Jer dečja je sreća poput leptira,
okrilje porodice je mesto gde se uživa i najlepše sniva…
Za dečju sreću, potrebno je jako malo,
a to malo u dve bi reči stalo…
Ono – Volim te- što svima prija podjednako
zagrljaj i mnoštvo nežnosti
za kojim se čežne jako…
Jer detetu roditeljska ljubav mnogo znači
uz podršku i sigurnost,
postaje se sigurniji i jači…

Čuvajmo Našu Planetu

Čuvajmo našu planetu
Svetlu budućnost svakom detetu
Na kojoj će moći srećno da raste
Da pogledom prati let laste,
Da kroči na zemlji bez straha
S optimizmom, bez pretnji i kraha…
Čuvajmo našu planetu
Ona je jedini dom celom svetu
U kojoj se pružaju divne bašte,
Ostvaruju snovi, čarolije mašte…
Čuvajmo našu planetu,
Let leptira na šarenom cvetu,
Plavi svod i vode plave,
Livade cvetne, mirisave…
Čuvajmo planetu, nema nam druge
Ona predstavlja život za sve ljude,
Čuvajmo je ko vazduh koji se udiše
Zbog svega onog što živi,
i još mnogo toga više…
Čuvajmo planetu, sa njom sebe
Bez nje vrednosti druge ništa ne vrede…
Čuvajmo našu planetu
budućnost čovečanstvu, svetu,
svako na nju podjednaka prava ima
da je čuva, uživa i majkom naziva.

Samo Dete

Dečiji je svet čudesan
U njemu se svašta ume,
Dovoljan je osmeh,
Pružena ruka,
Tuga se u oku bez reči razume.
Sve je lepo na svoj način
Život ima svoju draž,
Ume da sve uvaži
Da oprosti laž.
U tom svetu sreća vlada
Cvet mami usnulu pčelu,
Svaka mu je latica draga
I klovn u smešnom odelu.
Čarobne su reči ljubavi
koje nežno nesporazume ruše,
Očaravajući je u očima svod plav
Kao i samo prostranstvo
dečije duše.
Dečiji svet je čudesan
U njemu se može svašta,
Zanimljiv je na svoj način
svaki dan,
neprocenjivi doprinos
tome je dečija mašta.
Samo dete može
uživati u tom svetu
da ga prisustvom ulepšava,
jer čarolija toga sveta je mašta
u neiscrpna ljubav prava...

Šolkotović Snežana

Dr. Brajesh Kumar Gupta

Dr. Brajesh Kumar Gupta

Dr. Brajesh Kumar Gupta "Mewadev" is awarded honorary doctorate **"DOCTOR OF LITERATURE"** (DOCTOR HONORIS CAUSE) from THE INSTITUTE OF THE EUROPEAN ROMA STUDIES AND RESEARCH INTO CRIME AGAINST HUMANITY AND INTERNATIONAL LAW – BELGRADE (THE REPUBLIC OF SERBIA) and from "BRAZIL INTERNATIONAL COUNCIL CONIPA AND ITMUT INSTITUTE". He has been received Uttar Pradesh Gaurav Samman 2019. He is also winner of "Golden Book of World Records" and award winner of "Kavya Ratna Award" from "The Literati Cosmos Society (Reg. 75/2018-19)" – Mathura, U. P. (India) and "The Phrasal King Arbind Choudhary National Poetry Award- 2018" and one of member of Members of "Board of International Writers Association". He is also Ambassador of Humanity and manager of the organization named "Hafrikan Prince Art World" (HPAW - It is a brand name of the promotion of contemporary art) in the service of promoting the safety of humanity through art and culture. He is also III° "SECRETARY GENERAL OF THE WORLD UNION OF POETS" OF THE HISTORY OF THE WORLD UNION OF POETS FOR THE YEAR 2020. He is founder president of "CONTEMPORARY LITERARY SOCIETY OF AMLOR – BANDA (U.P. - India). He is editor, translator and reviewer par excellence. [...]

I Cry With Fear

We lived in the remains of ruined buildings
The people who live here seem to be passing through
There still city in ruins, sky fill with darkness
My heart hurts for relief

A chaotic collapse inside myself that I could never
My heart in ruins, my mind is a mess
Ascending the steps, to the withered old door,
Silent weeps of soul at the altar of peace

Resting and muddy from childhood play
Sunshine is gone, I only see grey
Most of all oblivious to errors and flaws
Blood and dirt, there is no shine

Insanity is creeping, at the brink
Don't know what I was thinking
No time to mourn, no place for tears
Burnt and charred past hope

Standing among the ruins of my dreams
Humanity is gone, replaced with stench
Honestly, I'm frightened and scared,
Take care of our children, and so is my will.

You Come From A Guilt

How should I let guilt consume you?
You are a darkened soul today?
The amiable dawn wishing me
Like to one more solace in the hope this day?
Or guilt-ridden that why found in the darkest corner of thoughts,
The nightmares that interferes with your expressions
A false man doesn't let go because you seemed wary!
My spiritual experience some of my pain for you
Until I turned you from a guilt,
Darkened edge of slimy sheet over the purple clouds
I carve even when blocked out, these are your imaginations
Cool breeze remorse kicked in that moment, embraces my sigh
A Million fears of losing you dearly,
Explosion drenches sprang out behind hedges
No one would want to lose a new tomorrow!

Dream Of Freedom

Don't get me wrong it's all okay
Your days are not without a care or your nights
If it is an unjust law you would abolish,
Unworried of how to please
Aimless in freedom the feather flew
Aloft on a whisper and sigh
How freedom in this world is light
For we are an oasis
Except for displays of fallen grace
From here, we will rise
For the sake of our love life
For all to whom the power's given
Freedom is a pitiful beauty,
Ugly as sin, and as right as rain
Its foundation built on sacrifice
But this kind of freedom
We all seem to devalue
A lonely impulse of delight
But while freedom is never free,
Before my helpless sight,
Fumbling are we still in gloom to untie
And come to take it from us
We are free from everything
Without the formula of sound,
The pious mastery of song
With a heart that feels
All I want is freedom.

Umid
Najjari

Umid Najjari(Ümid Nəccari) was born in Tabriz on April 15, 1989. After graduation from the Islamic Azad University, Umid Najjari continued his education at Baku Eurasian University, the Faculty of Philology, in Azerbaijan in 2016.

He is the author of "Valley of Birds","Photo of the Dark" and "On the other Side of the Walls", books of poems, and some translated literary books.

He was awarded the Samad Behrangi Award in 2016. He was awarded the Ali bey Hosseinzadeh Award in 2019.

He is a member of the Union of Azerbaijani Writers (UAW) and the World Young Turkish Writers Union (WYTWU).

The flag of peace

The breezes come to use from our shadows,
The butterflies fly from our fingertips,
The fall was an old neighbor,
The leaves turned yellow,
The trees fell down,
When it left.

It's the season of rain, I write this poem?
Where the words are "forgotten"
Everybody a little like Sizief
We're all dead Gods "as Zoroaster used to say
Coming closer, the darkness of the alleys vanishes in street
lights
The lighted candles turn to torches

Writes somewhere!
Write that
The lie poems of the world come true in your writing
Let me say
I let open the widows of tomorrows
I believe that the sun shall rise from your hands

Let me say
And know that
Foggy days will come from music notes to the beauty
alleys of the city
When I call you the dreams of the kingfishers vanishes in
signals of the ships
You tell the soldiers with your glances
You say that
Nobody fires the sky
White clouds are the Peace flags of the skies

How the soldiers can know? How the politicians?
The shoeless child in war scenes
Calls her mom before calling God
Tell her
Many things are untold in this poem
When my heart pulses, the untold words pain there
It's the season of rains, I write this poem:
There is a path of one word from us to you.
In our world
Wordlessness kills more than thirst

In the atmosphere of loneliness

I'm so silent …
Like the air after the rain
Breathed me like air in your longs
And left me to others
I was vanished in the atmosphere of loneliness like air
I'm so silent …
The blood doesn't run in hear
The eyes don't intend to see
Your silence is like a glass of wine
Drinking it, the destiny of human sulks
Sulking dashes the hopes in dreams
Your silence is speechlessness
The life runs in the deaf ears of Beethoven
The Piano vanishes in in your fingers
The notes freeze in symphony
Do...
Re...
Sol...
Yeah, your silence steps in my left side
You speak in my left side, step by step
The bucket of dreams are tensioned
The sun turns to cancer on the tomorrows' forehead
Leaving seems easy,
I can vanish
I can go to front of the silence for dying
Just be silent for a verse
Only for one word …

It's called heart

Call my eyes from your eyes
Telegram me from your hands
Rain your glances on my thirsty ceiling
Rain and rain on my lonely villages
I call you from the blueness of the seas
From the loneliness of lonely rooms
Come, …
There is only one step from night to the day
Just forget the past
Forget your hands in my hands
Leave yourself here and forget yourself
There is only one breath away from today to tomorrow
Close your eyes in my eyes, just
Pour your voice to my throat
The candles are human fingers in darkness
They light the lonely rooms like human body
The name of the camera in twenty first century
Is collapse
Stand up please,
Be silent for one minute!
There is a martyr in me, called the Heart
There is a plain of cotton, called the Homeland,
The fish get tired in my body for anxiety
A river runs in my vessels called Excitement
The balconies are the Feast of Opposition here
Hang up please,
If you call the depression
You'll never hear anybody
My ways to you are blocked
There's red light on crosses to you
I rest on you
I wait for you

Remembering

our fallen soldiers of verse

Janet Perkins Caldwell

February 14, 1959 ~ September 20, 2016

Alan W. Jankowski

16 March 1961 ~ 10 March 2017

Now available

1 April 2020

World Healing World Peace 2020

Poets for Humanity

Inner Child Press

News

Poetry Posse Members

We are so excited to share and announce a few of the current books, as well as the new and upcoming books of some of our Poetry Posse authors.

On the following pages we present to you ...

Jackie Davis Allen

Gail Weston Shazor

hülya n. yılmaz

Nizar Sartawi

Faleeha Hassan

Fahredin Shehu

Caroline 'Ceri' Nazareno

Eliza Segiet

William S. Peters, Sr.

Now Available

www.innerchildpress.com

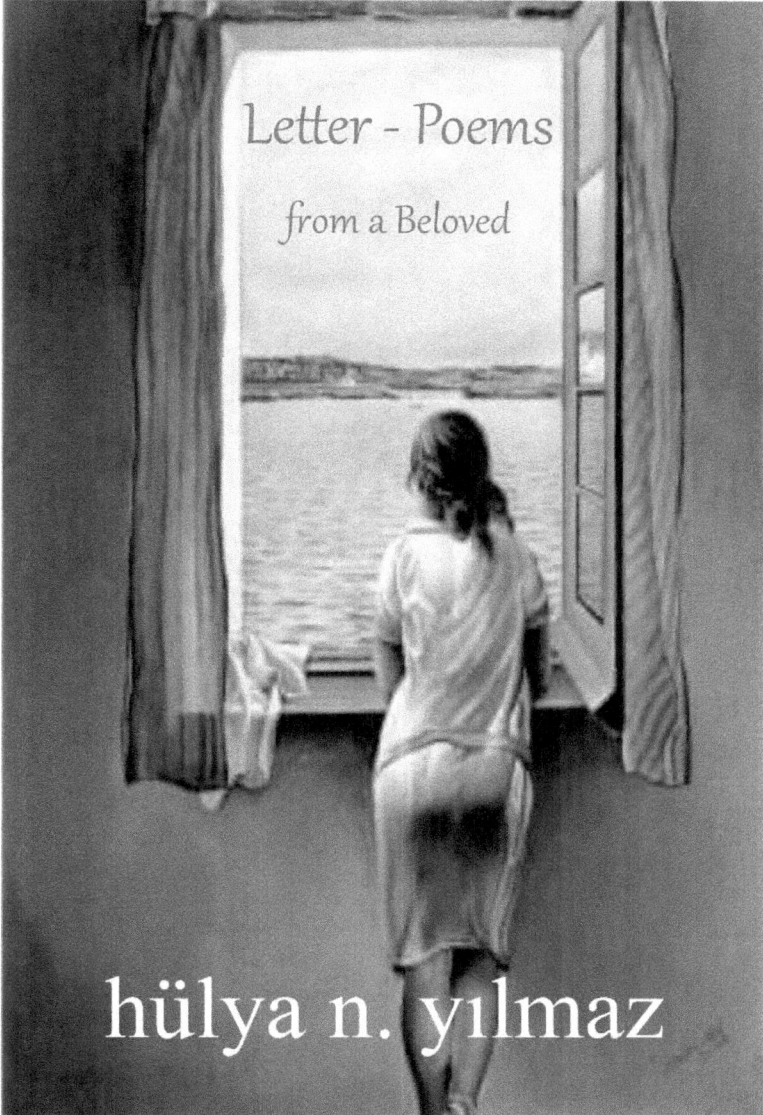

Letter - Poems

from a Beloved

hülya n. yılmaz

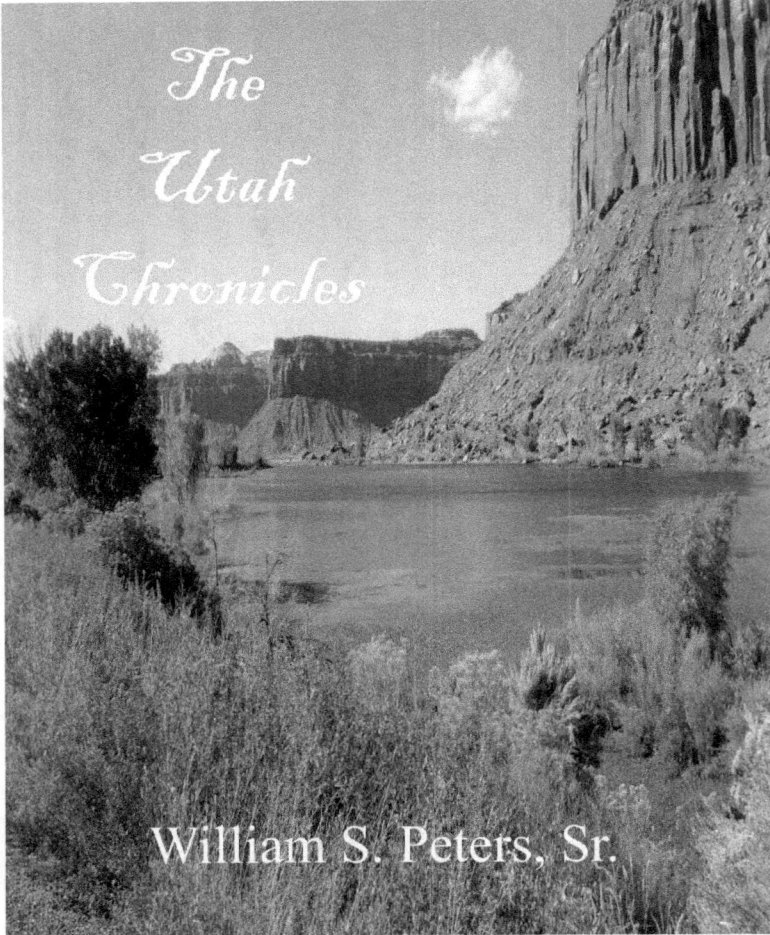

The Utah Chronicles

William S. Peters, Sr.

Now Available

www.innerchildpress.com

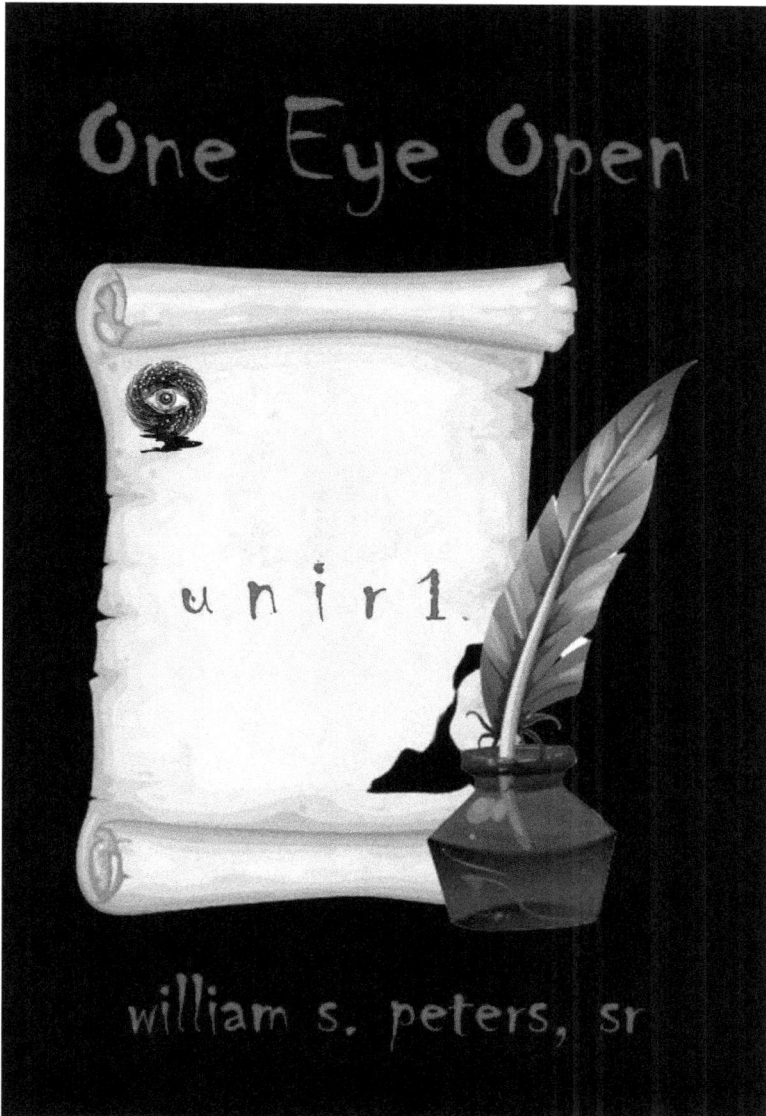

Inner Child Press News

COMING SOON

www.innerchildpress.com

The Book of krisar

volume v

william s. peters, sr.

Now Available

www.innerchildpress.com

The Book of krisar

Volume I

william s. peters, sr.

The Book of krisar

Volume II

william s. peters, sr.

Now Available

www.innerchildpress.com

The Book of krisar

Volume III

william s. peters, sr.

The Book of krisar

Volume IV

william s. peters, sr.

Now Available

www.innerchildpress.com

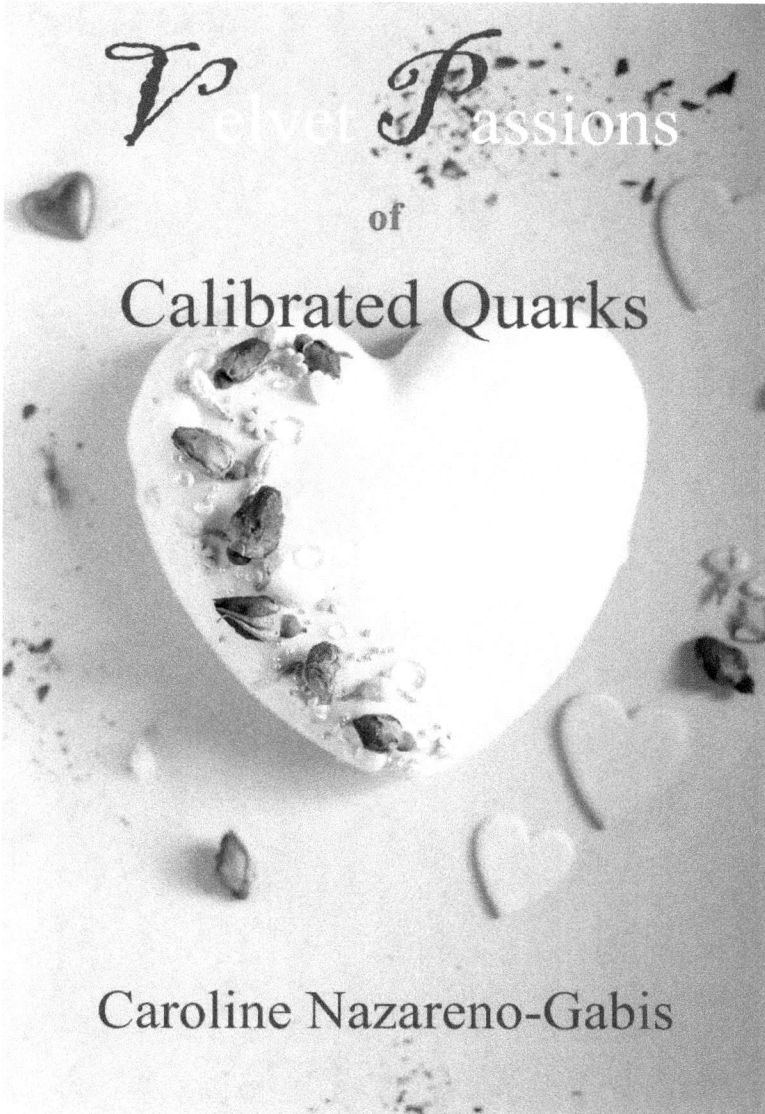

Velvet Passions

of

Calibrated Quarks

Caroline Nazareno-Gabis

Now Available

www.innerchildpress.com

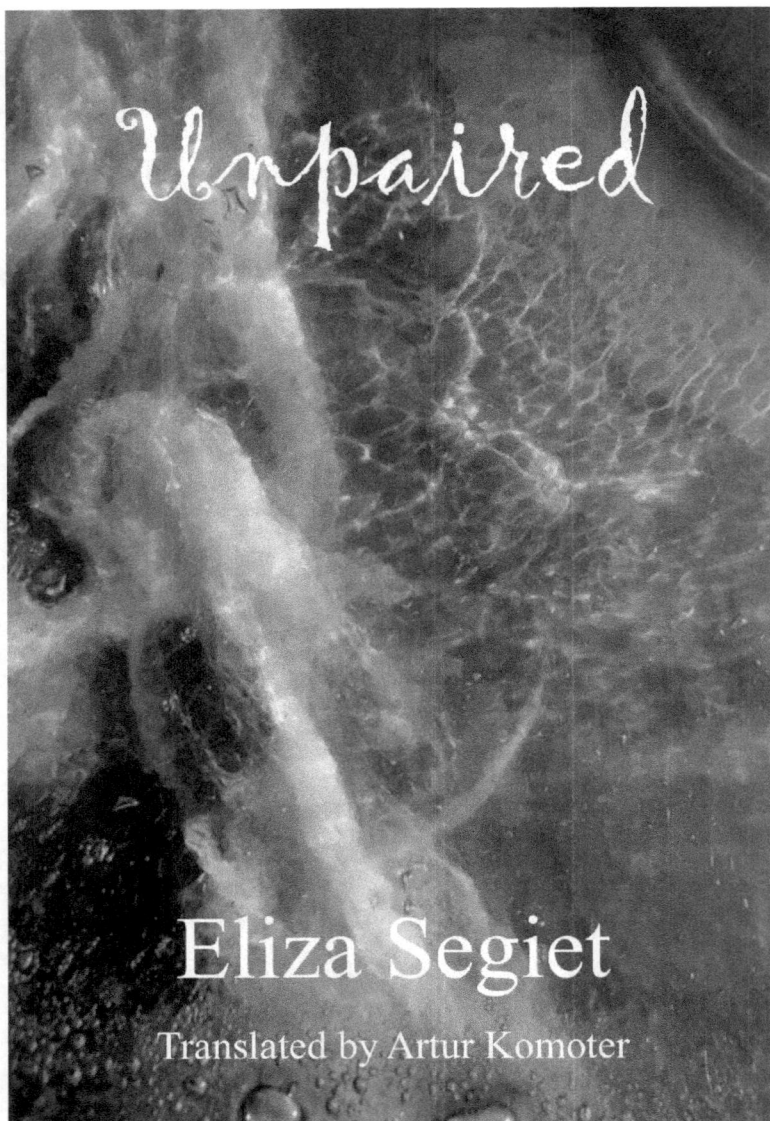

Unpaired

Eliza Segiet

Translated by Artur Komoter

Private Issue

www.innerchildpress.com

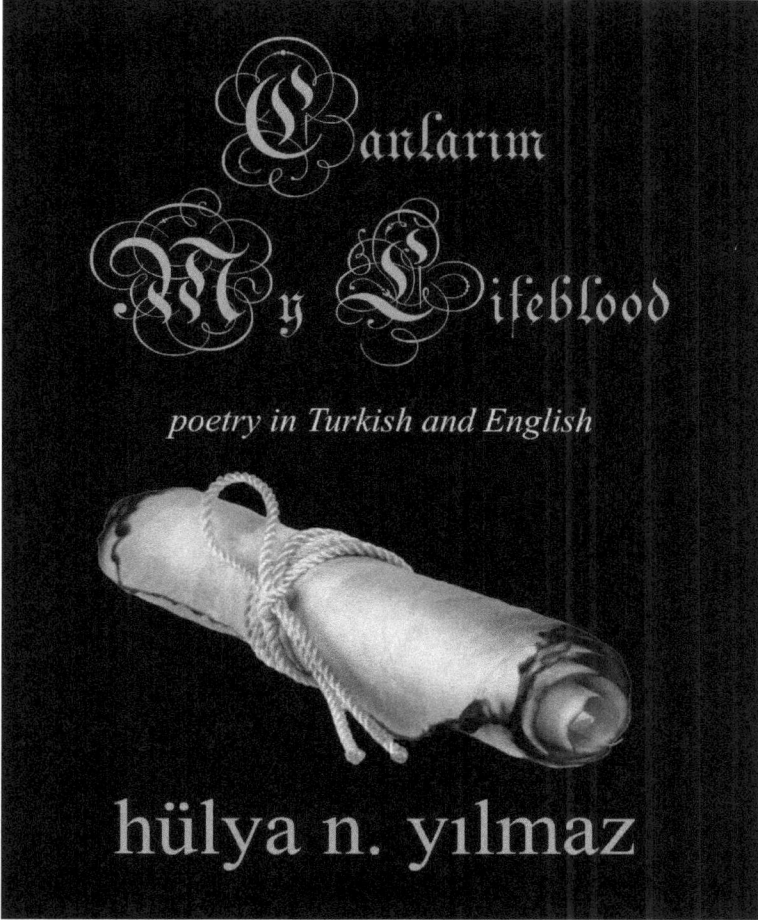

Canlarım

My Lifeblood

poetry in Turkish and English

hülya n. yılmaz

Now Available

www.innerchildpress.com

Butterfly's Voice

Faleeha Hassan

Translated by William M. Hutchins

Now Available at
www.innerchildpress.com

No Illusions

Through the Looking Glass

Jackie Davis Allen

Now Available at

www.innerchildpress.com

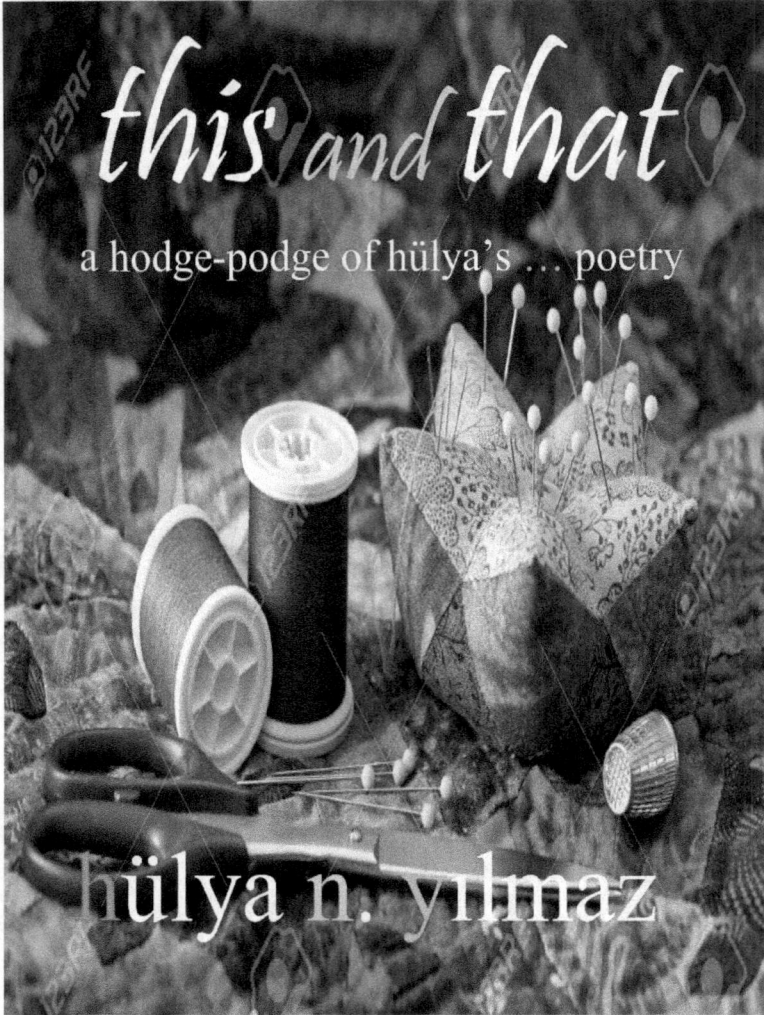

this and that

a hodge-podge of hülya's ... poetry

hülya n. yılmaz

Now Available at
www.innerchildpress.com

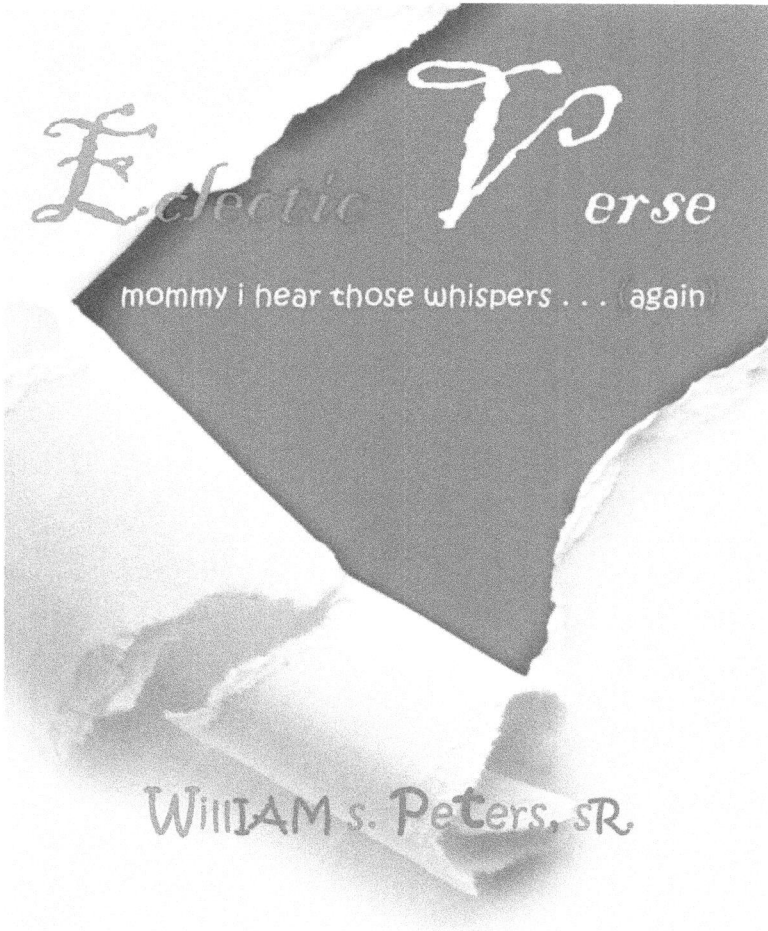

Eclectic Verse

mommy i hear those whispers . . . again

WilliAM s. PeTers, sR

HERENOW

◆

FAHREDIN SHEHU

Now Available at
www.innerchildpress.com

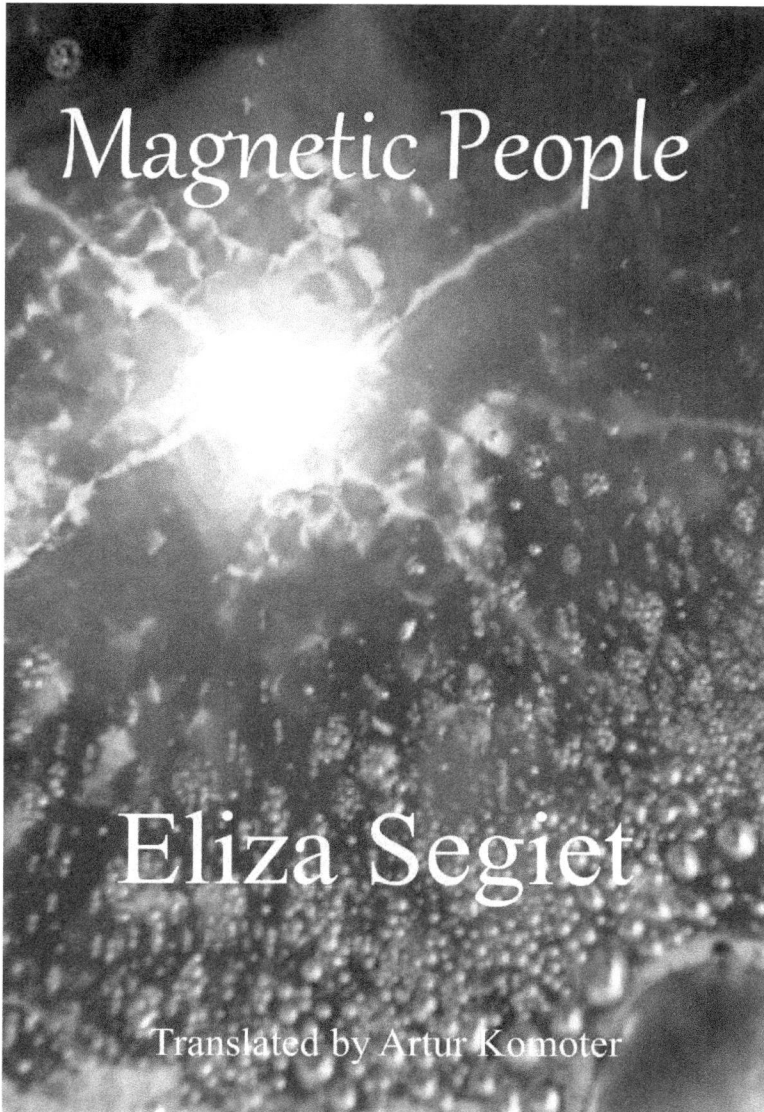

Magnetic People

Eliza Segiet

Translated by Artur Komoter

Now Available at
www.innerchildpress.com

Dark Side of the Moon

Jackie Davis Allen

Now Available at
www.innerchildpress.com

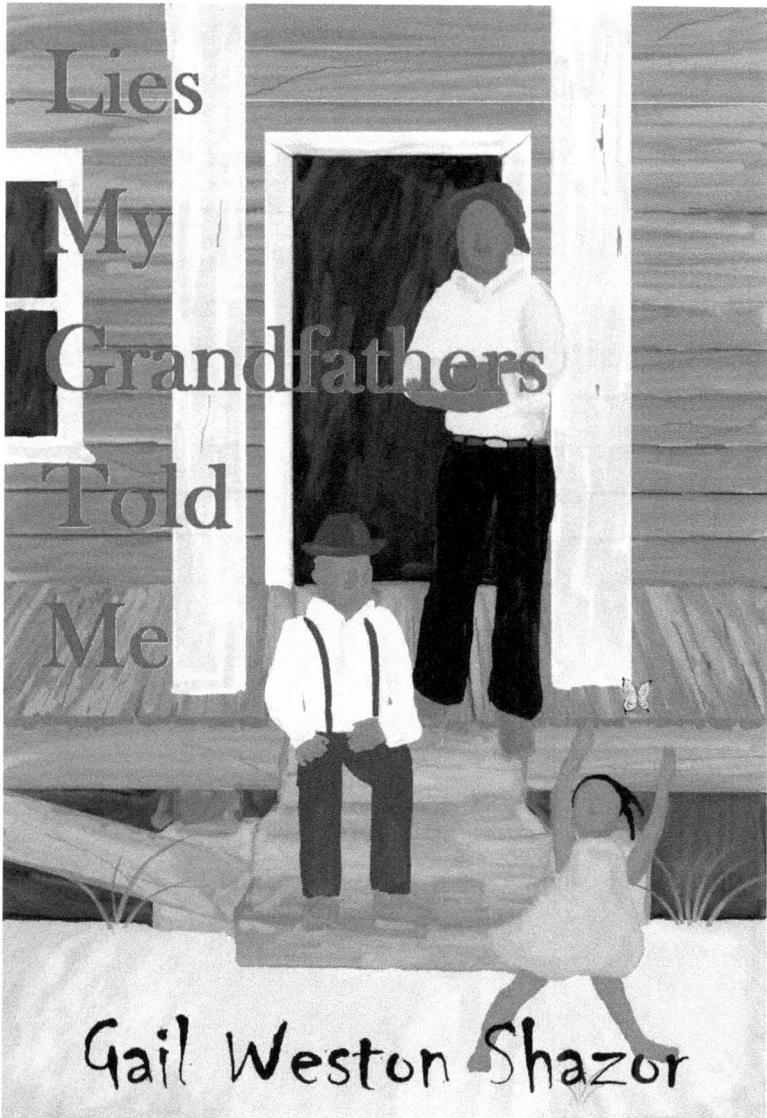

Lies
My
Grandfathers
Told
Me

Gail Weston Shazor

Now Available at
www.innerchildpress.com

Aflame

Memoirs in Verse

hülya n. yılmaz

Now Available at
www.innerchildpress.com

Now Available at
www.innerchildpress.com

Mass Graves

Faleeha Hassan

Now Available at
www.innerchildpress.com

Breakfast

for

Butterflies

Faleeha Hassan

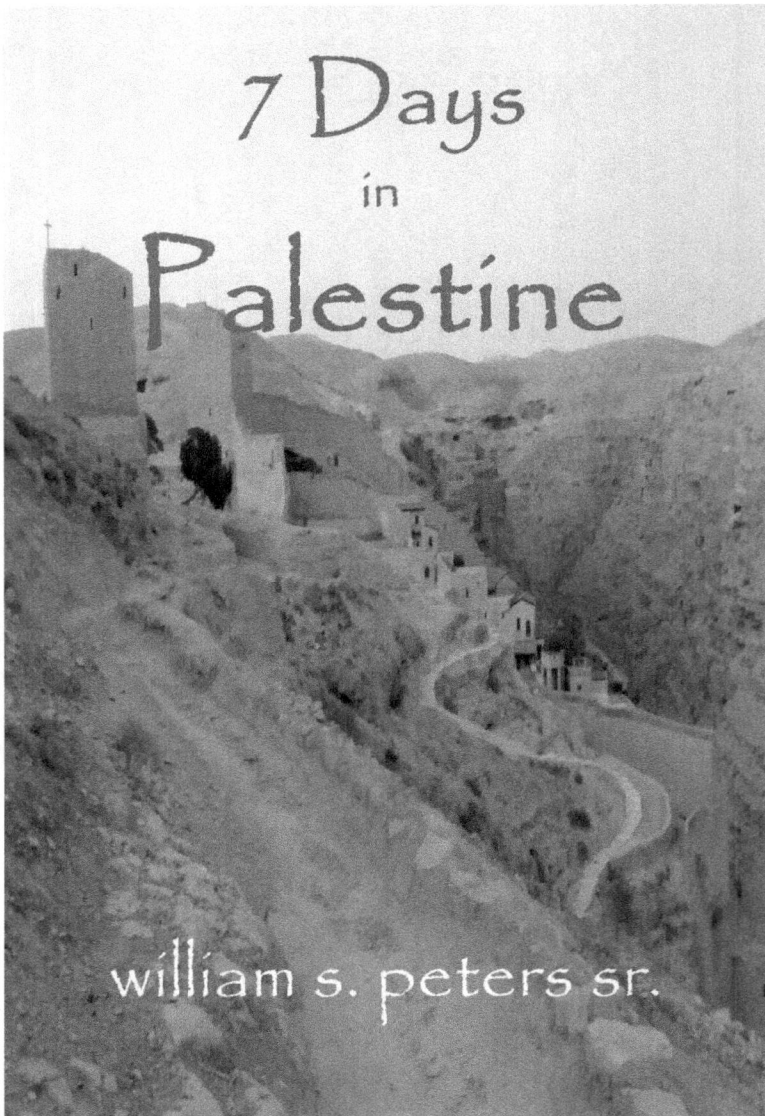

7 Days
in
Palestine

william s. peters sr.

Now Available at

www.innerchildpress.com

inner child press

presents

Tunisia My Love

william s. peters, sr.

Coming in the Summer of 2020

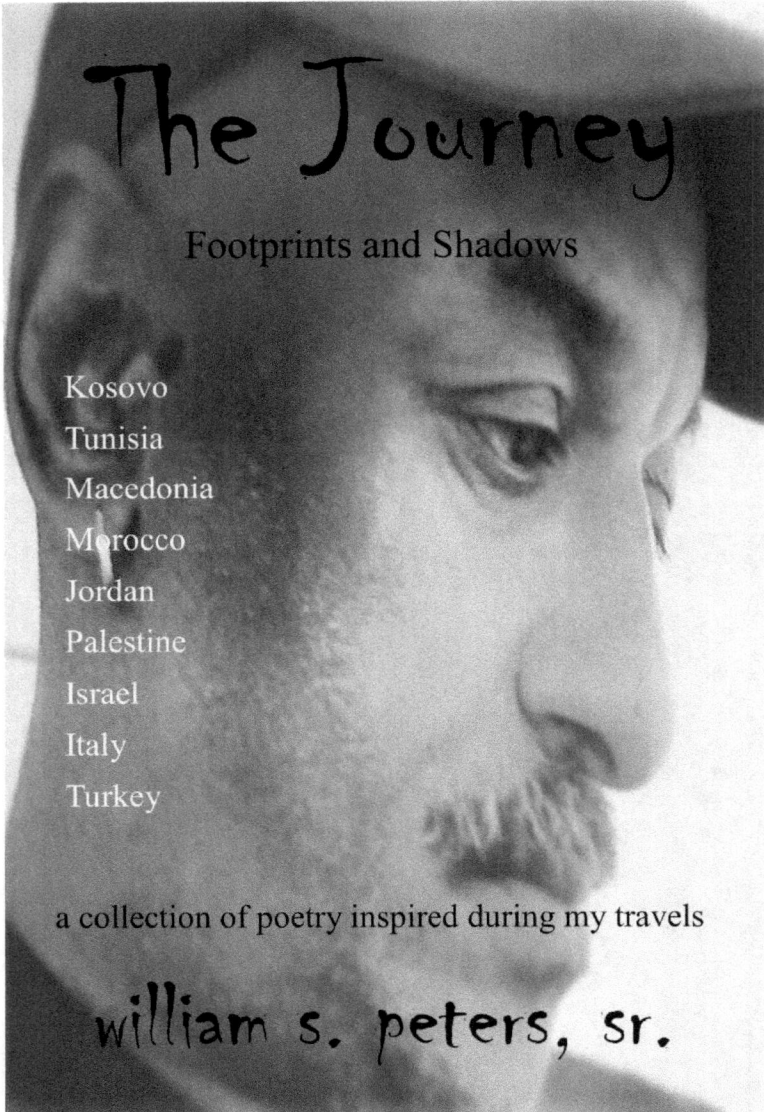

The Journey

Footprints and Shadows

Kosovo
Tunisia
Macedonia
Morocco
Jordan
Palestine
Israel
Italy
Turkey

a collection of poetry inspired during my travels

william s. peters, sr.

Now Available at
www.innerchildpress.com

Inward Reflections

Think on These Things
Book II

william s. peters, sr.

Other

Anthological

works from

Inner Child Press International

www.innerchildpress.com

Inner Child Press Anthologies

World Healing World Peace
2020

Poets for Humanity

Now Available

www.worldhealingworldpeacepoetry.com

Inner Child Press International

presents

W.A.R.

We Are Revolution

Poets for Humanity

COMING September 15th, 2020
www.innerchildpress.com

the Heart of a Poet

words for a better tomorrow

The Conscious Poets

Now Available

www.innerchildpress.com

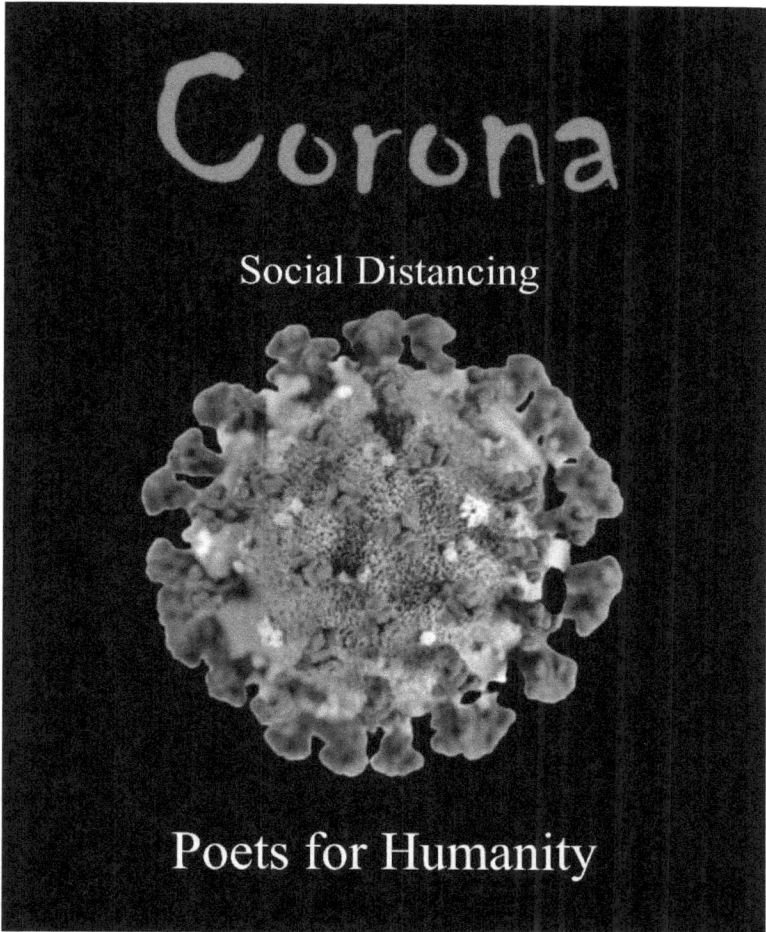

Corona

Social Distancing

Poets for Humanity

Now Available
www.innerchildpress.com

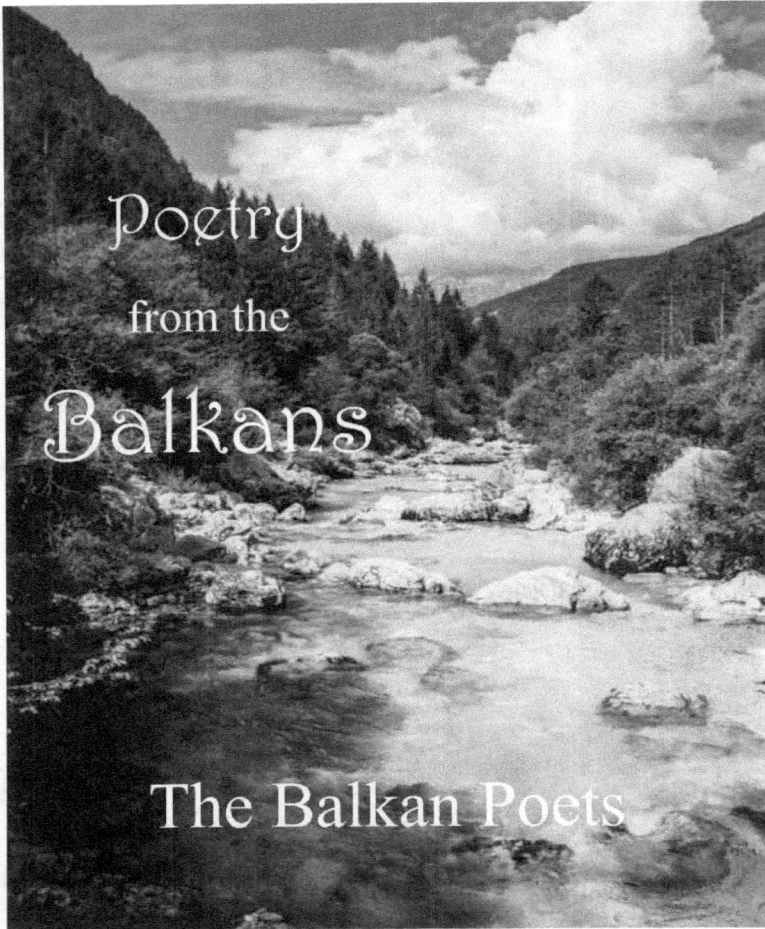

Poetry
from the
Balkans

The Balkan Poets

Now Available at
www.innerchildpress.com

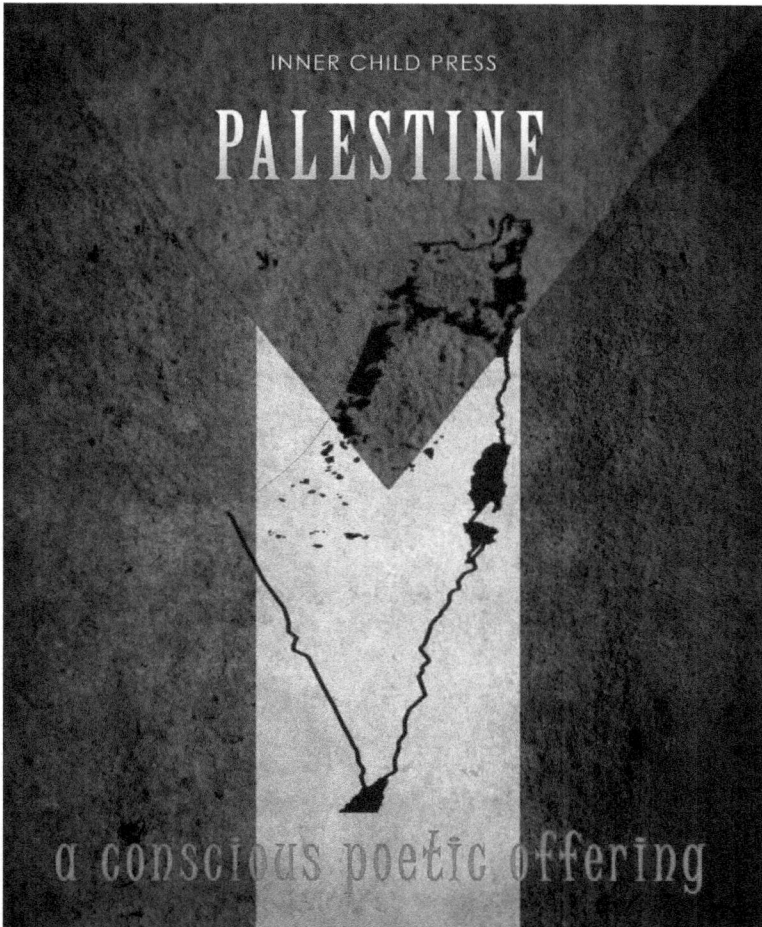

INNER CHILD PRESS

PALESTINE

a conscious poetic offering

Now Available at
www.innerchildpress.com

Now Available at

www.innerchildpress.com

Inner Child Press International
presents

A Love Anthology

2019

The Love Poets

Now Available

www.worldhealingworldpeacepoetry.com

Now Available

www.worldhealingworldpeacepoetry.com

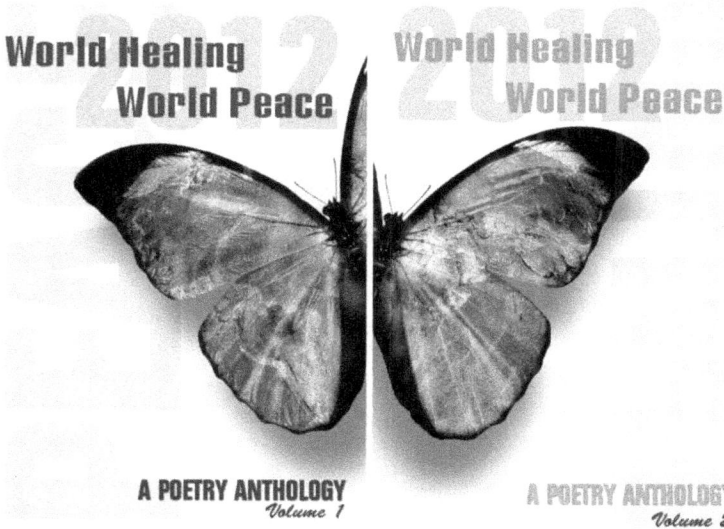

Now Available

www.worldhealingworldpeacepoetry.com

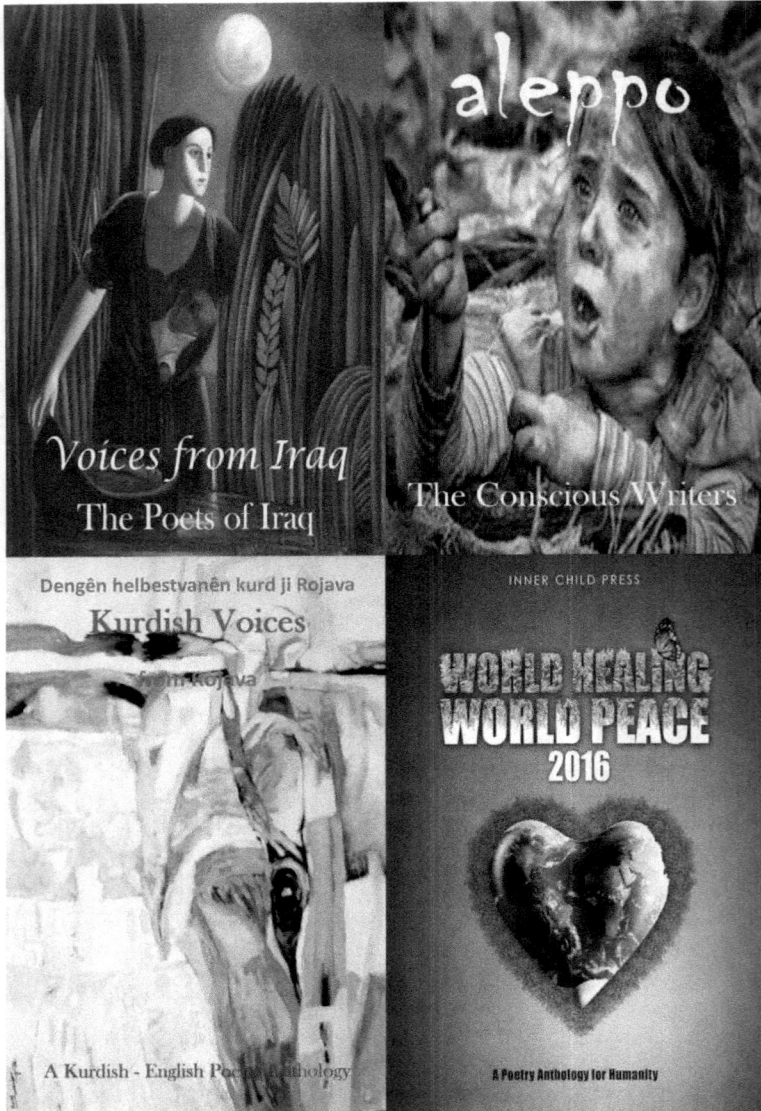

Now Available

www.innerchildpress.com/anthologies

Mandela

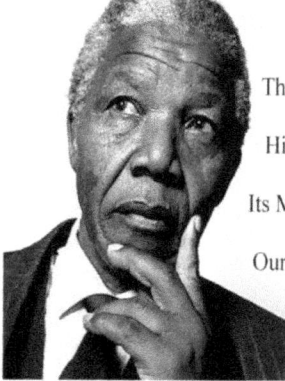

The Man

His Life

Its Meaning

Our Words

Poetry . . . Commentary & Stories
The Anthological Writers

A GATHERING OF WORDS

POETRY & COMMENTARY
FOR
TRAYVON MARTIN

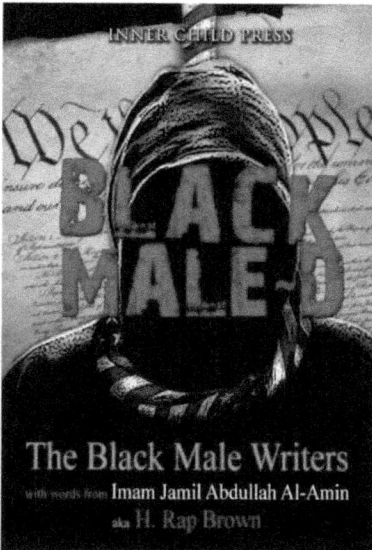

The Black Male Writers
with words from **Imam Jamil Abdullah Al-Amin**
aka **H. Rap Brown**

I
want
my
poetry
to . . . *volume* 4

the conscious poets
inspired by . . . Monte Smith

Now Available

Now Available

www.innerchildpress.com/anthologies

Now Available

www.innerchildpress.com/anthologies

191

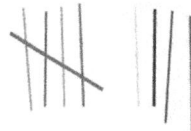

Now Available

www.innerchildpress.com/anthologies

Now Available

www.innerchildpress.com/the-year-of-the-poet

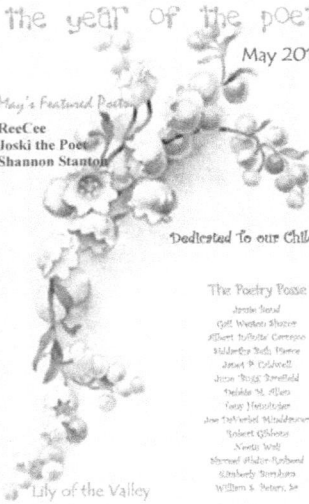

the year of the poet
May 2014

May's Featured Poets
ReeCee
Joski the Poet
Shannon Stanton

Dedicated to our Children

The Poetry Posse

Jamie Bond
Gail Weston Shazor
Albert Infinite Carrasco
Siddartha Beth Pierce
Janet P. Caldwell
June 'Bugg' Benefield
Debbie M. Allen
Gary Metzelaar
Joe DeVerbal Minddancer
Robert GNotes
Neetu Wali
Shareef Abdur-Rasheed
Kimberly Burnham
William S. Peters, Sr.

Lily of the Valley

the Year of the Poet
June 2014

Love & Relationship

Rose

June's Featured Poets
Shantelle McLin
Jacqueline D. E. Kennedy
Abraham N. Benjamin

The Poetry Posse
Jamie Bond
Gail Weston Shazor
Albert Infinite Carrasco
Siddartha Beth Pierce
Janet P. Caldwell
June 'Bugg' Benefield
Debbie M. Allen
Tony Henninger
Joe DeVerbal Minddancer
Robert Gibbons
Neetu Wali
Shareef Abdur-Rasheed
Kimberly Burnham
William S. Peters, Sr.

The Year of the Poet
July 2014

July Feature Poets
Christena A. V. Williams
Dr. John R. Strum
Rolande Otanrewaju Freedom

The Poetry Posse
Jamie Bond
Gail Weston Shazor
Albert Infinite Carrasco
Siddartha Beth Pierce
Janet P. Caldwell
June 'Bugg' Benefield
Debbie M. Allen
Tony Henninger
Joe DeVerbal Minddancer
Robert Gibbons
Neetu Wali
Shareef Abdur-Rasheed
Kimberly Burnham
William S. Peters, Sr.

Lotus
Asian Flower of the Month

The Year of the Poet
August 2014

Gladiolus

The Poetry Posse
Jamie Bond
Gail Weston Shazor
Albert Infinite Carrasco
Siddartha Beth Pierce
Janet P. Caldwell
June 'Bugg' Benefield
Debbie M. Allen
Tony Henninger
Joe DeVerbal Minddancer
Robert Gibbons
Neetu Wali
Shareef Abdur-Rasheed
Kimberly Burnham
William S. Peters, Sr.

August Feature Poets
Ann White * Rosalind Cherry * Shelia Jenkins

Now Available

www.innerchildpress.com/the-year-of-the-poet

194

The Year of the Poet
September 2014

Aster   Morning-Glory

Wild Child for September Birth Flower

September Feature Poets
Florence Malone ● Keith Alan Hamilton

The Poetry Posse
Jamie Bond ● Gail Weston Shazor ● Albert InfiniteCarrasco ● Siddartha Beth Pierce
Janet P. Caldwell ● June 'Bugg' Barefield ● Debbie M. Allen ● Tony Henninger
Joe DaVerbal Minddancer ● Robert Gibbons ● Neetu Wali ● Shareef Abdur-Rasheed
Kimberly Burnham ● William S. Peters, Sr.

THE YEAR OF THE POET
October 2014

Red Poppy

The Poetry Posse
Jamie Bond ● Gail Weston Shazor ● Albert InfiniteCarrasco ● Siddartha Beth Pierce
Janet P. Caldwell ● June 'Bugg' Barefield ● Debbie M. Allen ● Tony Henninger
Joe DaVerbal Minddancer ● Robert Gibbons ● Neetu Wali ● Shareef Abdur-Rasheed
Kimberly Burnham ● William S. Peters, Sr.

October Feature Poets
Ceri Naz ● Rajendra Padhi ● Elizabeth Castillo

THE YEAR OF THE POET
November 2014

Chrysanthemum

The Poetry Posse
Jamie Bond ● Gail Weston Shazor ● Albert InfiniteCarrasco ● Siddartha Beth Pierce
Janet P. Caldwell ● June 'Bugg' Barefield ● Debbie M. Allen ● Tony Henninger
Joe DaVerbal Minddancer ● Robert Gibbons ● Neetu Wali ● Shareef Abdur-Rasheed
Kimberly Burnham ● William S. Peters, Sr.

November Feature Poets
Jocelyn Mosman ● Jackie Allen ● James Moore ● Neville Hiatt

THE YEAR OF THE POET
December 2014

Jamie Bond
Gail Weston Shazor
Albert InfiniteCarrasco
Siddartha Beth Pierce
Janet P. Caldwell
June 'Bugg' Barefield
Debbie M. Allen
Tony Henninger
Joe DaVerbal Minddancer
Robert Gibbons
Neetu Wali
Shareef Abdur-Rasheed
Kimberly Burnham
William S. Peters, Sr.

Narcissus

December Feature Poets
Katherine Wyatt ● Writtential ● Santosh Bakaya ● Justin Blake

Now Available

www.innerchildpress.com/the-year-of-the-poet

THE YEAR OF THE POET II
January 2015

Garnet

The Poetry Posse

Jamie Bond
Gail Weston Shazor
Albert 'Infinite' Carrasco
Siddartha Beth Pierce
Janet P. Caldwell
Tony Henninger
Joe DaVerbal Minddancer
Robert Gibbons
Neetu Wali
Shareef Abdur – Rasheed
Kimberly Burnham
Ann White
Keith Alan Hamilton
Katherine Wyatt
Fahredin Shehu
Hülya N. Yılmaz
Teresa E. Gallion
Jackie Allen
William S. Peters, Sr.

January Feature Poets
Bismay Mohanti * Jen Walls * Eric Judah

THE YEAR OF THE POET II
February 2015

Amethyst

THE POETRY POSSE

Jamie Bond
Gail Weston Shazor
Albert 'Infinite' Carrasco
Siddartha Beth Pierce
Janet P. Caldwell
Tony Henninger
Joe DaVerbal Minddancer
Robert Gibbons
Neetu Wali
Shareef Abdur – Rasheed
Kimberly Burnham
Ann White
Keith Alan Hamilton
Katherine Wyatt
Fahredin Shehu
Hülya N. Yılmaz
Teresa E. Gallion
Jackie Allen
William S. Peters, Sr.

FEBRUARY FEATURE POETS
Iram Fatima * Bob McNeil * Kerstin Centervall

The Year of the Poet II
March 2015

Our Featured Poets
Heung Sook * Anthony Arnold * Alicia Poland

Bloodstone

The Poetry Posse 2015
Jamie Bond * Gail Weston Shazor * Albert 'Infinite' Carrasco
Siddartha Beth Pierce * Janet P. Caldwell * Tony Henninger
Joe DaVerbal Minddancer * Neetu Wali * Shareef Abdur – Rasheed
Kimberly Burnham * Ann White * Keith Alan Hamilton
Katherine Wyatt * Fahredin Shehu * Hülya N. Yılmaz
Teresa E. Gallion * Jackie Allen * William S. Peters, Sr.

The Year of the Poet II
April 2015

Celebrating International Poetry Month

Our Featured Poets
Raja Williams * Dennis Ferado * Laure Charazac

Diamonds

The Poetry Posse 2015
Jamie Bond * Gail Weston Shazor * Albert 'Infinite' Carrasco
Siddartha Beth Pierce * Janet P. Caldwell * Tony Henninger
Joe DaVerbal Minddancer * Neetu Wali * Shareef Abdur – Rasheed
Kimberly Burnham * Ann White * Keith Alan Hamilton
Katherine Wyatt * Fahredin Shehu * Hülya N. Yılmaz
Teresa E. Gallion * Jackie Allen * William S. Peters, Sr.

Now Available

www.innerchildpress.com/the-year-of-the-poet

The Year of the Poet II
May 2015

May's Featured Poets

Geri Algeri
Akin Mosi Chinnery
Anna Jakubcza

Emeralds

The Poetry Posse 2015

Jamie Bond * Gail Weston Shazor * Albert 'Infinite' Carrasco
Siddartha Beth Pierce * Janet P. Caldwell * Tony Henninger
Joe DaVerbal Minddancer * Neetu Wali * Shareef Abdur - Rasheed
Kimberly Burnham * Ann White * Keith Alan Hamilton
Katherine Wyatt * Fahredin Shehu * Hülya N. Yilmaz
Teresa E. Gallion * Jackie Allen * William S. Peters. Sr.

The Year of the Poet II
June 2015

June's Featured Poets

Andút Arustomyan * Yvette D. Murrell * Regina A. Walker

Pearl

The Poetry Posse 2015

Jamie Bond * Gail Weston Shazor * Albert 'Infinite' Carrasco
Siddartha Beth Pierce * Janet P. Caldwell * Tony Henninger
Joe DaVerbal Minddancer * Neetu Wali * Shareef Abdur – Rasheed
Kimberly Burnham * Ann White * Keith Alan Hamilton
Katherine Wyatt * Fahredin Shehu * Hülya N. Yilmaz
Teresa E. Gallion * Jackie Allen * William S. Peters. Sr

The Year of the Poet II
July 2015

The Featured Poets for July 2015

Abhik Shome * Christina Neal * Robert Neal

Rubies

The Poetry Posse 2015

Jamie Bond * Gail Weston Shazor * Albert 'Infinite' Carrasco
Siddartha Beth Pierce * Janet P. Caldwell * Tony Henninger
Joe DaVerbal Minddancer * Neetu Wali * Shareef Abdur – Rasheed
Kimberly Burnham * Ann White * Keith Alan Hamilton
Katherine Wyatt * Fahredin Shehu * Hülya N. Yilmaz
Teresa E. Gallion * Jackie Allen * William S. Peters. Sr.

The Year of the Poet II
August 2015

Peridot

Featured Poets

Gayle Howell
Ann Chalasz
Christopher Schultz

The Poetry Posse 2015

Jamie Bond * Gail Weston Shazor * Albert 'Infinite' Carrasco
Siddartha Beth Pierce * Janet P. Caldwell * Tony Henninger
Joe DaVerbal Minddancer * Neetu Wali * Shareef Abdur – Rasheed
Kimberly Burnham * Ann White * Keith Alan Hamilton
Katherine Wyatt * Fahredin Shehu * Hülya N. Yilmaz
Teresa E. Gallion * Jackie Allen * William S. Peters. Sr

Now Available

www.innerchildpress.com/the-year-of-the-poet

The Year of the Poet II
September 2015

Featured Poets
Alfreda Ghee   Lonneice Weeks Badley   Demetrios Trifiatis

Sapphires

The Poetry Posse 2015

Jamie Bond * Gail Weston Shazor * Albert 'Infinite' Carrasco
Siddartha Beth Pierce * Janet P. Caldwell * Tony Henninger
Joe DaVerbal Minddancer * Neetu Wali * Shareef Abdur – Rasheed
Kimberly Burnham * Ann White * Keith Alan Hamilton
Katherine Wyatt * Fahredin Shehu * Hülya N. Yılmaz
Teresa E. Gallion * Jackie Allen * William S. Peters. Sr.

The Year of the Poet II
October 2015

Featured Poets
Monte Smith * Laura J. Wolfe * William Washington

Opal

The Poetry Posse 2015

Jamie Bond * Gail Weston Shazor * Albert 'Infinite' Carrasco
Siddartha Beth Pierce * Janet P. Caldwell * Tony Henninger
Joe DaVerbal Minddancer * Neetu Wali * Shareef Abdur – Rasheed
Kimberly Burnham * Ann White * Keith Alan Hamilton
Katherine Wyatt * Fahredin Shehu * Hülya N. Yılmaz
Teresa E. Gallion * Jackie Allen * William S. Peters. Sr.

The Year of the Poet II
November 2015

Featured Poets
Alan W. Jankowski
Bismay Mohanty
James Moore

Topaz

The Poetry Posse 2015

Jamie Bond * Gail Weston Shazor * Albert 'Infinite' Carrasco
Siddartha Beth Pierce * Janet P. Caldwell * Tony Henninger
Joe DaVerbal Minddancer * Neetu Wali * Shareef Abdur – Rasheed
Kimberly Burnham * Ann White * Keith Alan Hamilton
Katherine Wyatt * Fahredin Shehu * Hülya N. Yılmaz
Teresa E. Gallion * Jackie Allen * William S. Peters. Sr.

The Year of the Poet II
December 2015

Featured Poets
Kerione Bryan * Michelle Joan Barulich * Neville Hiatt

Turquoise

The Poetry Posse 2015

Jamie Bond * Gail Weston Shazor * Albert 'Infinite' Carrasco
Siddartha Beth Pierce * Janet P. Caldwell * Tony Henninger
Joe DaVerbal Minddancer * Neetu Wali * Shareef Abdur – Rasheed
Kimberly Burnham * Ann White * Keith Alan Hamilton
Katherine Wyatt * Fahredin Shehu * Hülya N. Yılmaz
Teresa E. Gallion * Jackie Allen * William S. Peters. Sr.

Now Available

www.innerchildpress.com/the-year-of-the-poet

The Year of the Poet III
January 2016

Featured Poets

Lana Joseph * Atom Cyrus Rush * Christena Williams

Dark-eyed Junco

The Poetry Posse 2016

The Year of the Poet III
February 2016

Featured Poets

Anthony Arnold
Anna Chalasz
De Andre Hawthorne

Puffin

The Poetry Posse 2016

The Year of the Poet
March 2016
Featured Poets

Jeton Kelmendi   Nizar Sartawi   Sami Muhanna

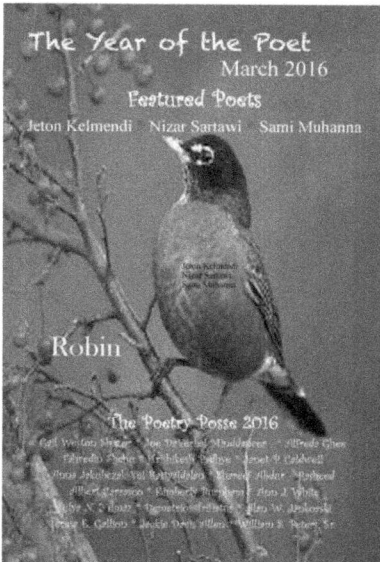

Robin

The Poetry Posse 2016

The Year of the Poet III

Featured Poets

Ali Abdolrezaei

Anna Chalasz

Agim Vinca

Ceri Naz

Black Capped Chickadee

The Poetry Posse 2016

celebrating international poetry month

Now Available

www.innerchildpress.com/the-year-of-the-poet

199

The Year of the Poet
May 2016

Bob Strum
Barbara Allan
D.L. Davis

Oriole

The Year of the Poet III
June 2016

Featured Poets

Qibrije Demiri- Frangu
Naime Beqiraj
Faleeha Hassan
Bedri Zyberaj

Black Necked Stilt

The Poetry Posse 2016

The Year of the Poet II
July 2016

Tram Fatima 'Ashi
Langley Shazor
Jody Doty
Emilia T. Davis

Indigo Bunting

The Poetry Posse 2016

The Year of the Poet III
August 2016

Featured Poets

Anita Dash
Irena Jovanovic
Malgorzata Gouluda

Painted Bunting

The Poetry Posse 2016

Now Available

www.innerchildpress.com/the-year-of-the-poet

The Year of the Poet III
September 2016

Featured Poets

Simone Weber
Abhijit Sen
Eunice Barbara C. Novio

Long Billed Curlew

The Poetry Posse 2016

The Year of the Poet III
October 2016

Featured Poets

Luna Joseph
Kumarendra Krishnamurthy R
James Moore

Barn Owl

The Poetry Posse 2016

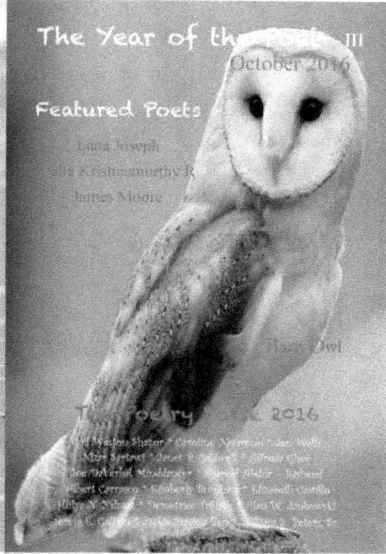

The Year of the Poet III
November 2016

Featured Poets

Rosemary Burns
Robin Ouzman Hislop
Lonneice Weeks-Badley

Northern Cardinal

The Poetry Posse 2016

Gail Weston Shazor * Caroline Nazareno * Jen Walls
Mize Sertawi * Janet P. Caldwell * Alfreda Ghee
Joe DeVerhal Minddancer * Shareef Abdur - Rasheed
Albert Carrasco * Kimberly Burnham * Elizabeth Castillo
Hülya N. Yılmaz * Demetrios Trifiatis * Fllen W. Jaskowski
Teresa E. Gallion * Jackie Davis Allen * William S. Peters, Sr.

The Year of the Poet III
December 2016

Featured Poets

Samih Masoud
Mountassir Aziz Bien
Abdulkadir Musa

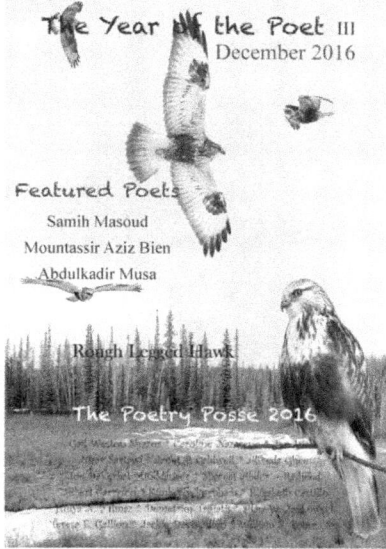

Rough Legged Hawk

The Poetry Posse 2016

Now Available

The Year of the Poet IV
January 2017

Featured Poets
Jon Winell
Natalie Shields
Irani Fatima Ashi

Quaking Aspen

The Poetry Posse 2017

The Year of the Poet IV
February 2017

Featured Poets
Lin Ross
Soukaina Fathi
Anwer Ghani

Witch Hazel

The Poetry Posse 2017

The Year of the Poet IV
March 2017

Featured Poets
Tremell Stevens
Francisca Ricinski
Jamil Abu Shaih

The Eastern Redbud

The Poetry Posse 2017

The Year of the Poet IV
April 2017

Featured Poets
Dr. Rachida Barman
Neptune Barman
Masood Khalaf

The Blossoming Cherry

The Poetry Posse 2017

Now Available

www.innerchildpress.com/the-year-of-the-poet

The Year of the Poet IV
May 2017

The Flowering Dogwood Tree

Featured Poets
Kallisa Powell
Alicja Maria Kuberska
Fethi Sassi

The Poetry Posse 2017

The Year of the Poet IV
June 2017

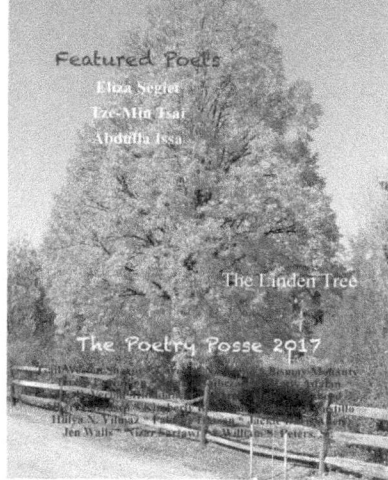

Featured Poets
Elisa Segiet
Tze-Min Tsai
Abdulla Issa

The Linden Tree

The Poetry Posse 2017

The Year of the Poet IV
July 2017

Featured Poets
Anca Mihaela Bruma
Ibaa Ismail
Zvonko Taneski

The Oak Moon

The Poetry Posse 2017

The Year of the Poet IV
August 2017

Featured Poets
Jonathan Aquino
Kitty Hsu
Langley Shazor

The Hazelnut Tree

The Poetry Posse 2017

Now Available

www.innerchildpress.com/the-year-of-the-poet

The Year of the Poet IV
September 2017

Featured Poets
Martina Reisz Newberry
Ameer Nassir
Christine Fulco Neal
Robert Neal

The Elm Tree

The Poetry Posse 2017

Gail Weston Shazor * Caroline Nazareno * Bismay Mohanty
Teresa E. Gallion * Anna Jakubczak Vel Ratty Adalan
Joe DaVerbal Minddancer * Shareef Abdur – Rasheed
Albert Carrasco * Kimberly Burnham * Elizabeth Castillo
Hülya N. Yılmaz * Faleeha Hassan * Jackie Davis Allen
Jen Walls * Nizar Sartawi * William S. Peters, Sr.

The Year of the Poet IV
October 2017

Featured Poets
Ahmed Abu Saleem
Nedal Al-Qaeim
Sadeddin Shahin

The Black Walnut Tree

The Poetry Posse 2017

Gail Weston Shazor * Caroline Nazareno * Bismay Mohanty
Teresa E. Gallion * Anna Jakubczak Vel Ratty Adalan
Joe DaVerbal Minddancer * Shareef Abdur – Rasheed
Albert Carrasco * Kimberly Burnham * Elizabeth Castillo
Hülya N. Yılmaz * Faleeha Hassan * Jackie Davis Allen
Jen Walls * Nizar Sartawi * * William S. Peters, Sr.

The Year of the Poet IV
November 2017

Featured Poets
Kay Peters
Alfreda D. Ghee
Gabriella Garofalo
Rosemary Cappello

The Tree of Life

The Poetry Posse 2017

Gail Weston Shazor * Caroline Nazareno * Bismay Mohanty
Teresa E. Gallion * Anna Jakubczak Vel Ratty Adalan
Joe DaVerbal Minddancer * Shareef Abdur – Rasheed
Albert Carrasco * Kimberly Burnham * Elizabeth Castillo
Hülya N. Yılmaz * Faleeha Hassan * Jackie Davis Allen
Jen Walls * Nizar Sartawi * William S. Peters, Sr.

The Year of the Poet IV
December 2017

Featured Poets
Justice Clarke
Mariel M. Pabroa
Kiley Brown

The Fig Tree

The Poetry Posse 2017

Gail Weston Shazor * Caroline Nazareno * Bismay Mohanty
Teresa E. Gallion * Anna Jakubczak Vel Ratty Adalan
Joe DaVerbal Minddancer * Shareef Abdur – Rasheed
Albert Carrasco * Kimberly Burnham * Elizabeth Castillo
Hülya N. Yılmaz * Faleeha Hassan * Jackie Davis Allen
Jen Walls * Nizar Sartawi * William S. Peters, Sr.

Now Available

www.innerchildpress.com/the-year-of-the-poet

The Year of the Poet V
January 2018
Featured Poets
Iyad Shamasnah
Yasmeen Hamzeh
Ali Abdolrezaei

Aksum

The Poetry Posse 2018
Gail Weston Shazor * Caroline Nazareno * Tezmin Ition Tsai
Hülya N. Yılmaz * Faleeha Hassan * Jackie Davis Allen
Teresa E. Gallion * Anna Jakubczak Vel Ratty Adalan
Alicja Maria Kubenska * Shareef Abdur – Rasheed
Kimberly Burnham * Elizabeth Castillo
Nizar Sartawi * William S. Peters, Sr.

The Year of the Poet V
February 2018

Sabean

Featured Poets
Muhammad Azrain
Anna Szawracka
Abhilipsa Kuanar
Aanika Aery

The Poetry Posse 2018
Gail Weston Shazor * Caroline Nazareno * Tezmin Ition Tsai
Hülya N. Yılmaz * Faleeha Hassan * Jackie Davis Allen
Teresa E. Gallion * Anna Jakubczak Vel Ratty Adalan
Alicja Maria Kubenska * Shareef Abdur – Rasheed
Kimberly Burnham * Elizabeth Castillo
Nizar Sartawi * William S. Peters, Sr.

The Year of the Poet V
March 2018

Featured Poets
Iram Fatima 'Ashi'
Cassandra Swan
Jaleel Khazaal
Shazia Zaman

Mexico   Cuba

Caribbean
&
Middle America

The Poetry Posse 2018
Gail Weston Shazor * Nizar Sartawi * Hülya N. Yılmaz
Jackie Davis Allen * Caroline 'Ceri' Nazareno
Alicja Maria Kubenska * Teresa E. Gallion
Faleeha Hassan * Shareef Abdur – Rasheed
Kimberly Burnham * Elizabeth Castillo
Tezmin Ition Tsai * William S. Peters, Sr.

The Year of the Poet V
April 2018

Featured Poets

The Nez Perce

The Poetry Posse 2018

Now Available

www.innerchildpress.com/the-year-of-the-poet

205

The Year of the Poet V
May 2018

Featured Poets

Zaldy Carreos de Leon Jr
Sylwia K. Malinowska
Claudia Abendi
Ofelia Fridan

The Sumerians

The Poetry Posse 2018

Gail Weston Shazor * Nizar Sartawi * Hülya N. Yılmaz
Jackie Davis Allen * Caroline 'Ceri' Nazareno
Alicja Maria Kuberska * Teresa E. Gallion
Kimberly Burnham * Shareef Abdur – Rasheed
Faleeha Hassan * Elizabeth Castillo * Swapna Behera
Tezmin Ition Tsai * William S. Peters, Sr.

The Year of the Poet V
June 2018

Featured Poets

Bilall Maliqi * Daim Miftari * Gojko Božović * Sofija Živković

The Paleo Indians

The Poetry Posse 2018

Gail Weston Shazor * Nizar Sartawi * Hülya N. Yılmaz
Jackie Davis Allen * Caroline 'Ceri' Nazareno
Alicja Maria Kuberska * Teresa E. Gallion
Kimberly Burnham * Shareef Abdur – Rasheed
Faleeha Hassan * Elizabeth Castillo * Swapna Behera
Tezmin Ition Tsai * William S. Peters, Sr.

The Year of the Poet V
July 2018

Featured Poets

Padmaja Iyengar-Paddy
Mohammad Ikbal Harb
Eliza Segiet
Tom Higgins

Oceania

The Poetry Posse 2018

Gail Weston Shazor * Nizar Sartawi * Hülya N. Yılmaz
Jackie Davis Allen * Caroline 'Ceri' Nazareno
Alicja Maria Kuberska * Teresa E. Gallion
Kimberly Burnham * Shareef Abdur – Rasheed
Faleeha Hassan * Elizabeth Castillo * Swapna Behera
Tezmin Ition Tsai * William S. Peters, Sr.

The Year of the Poet V
August 2018

Featured Poets

Hussein Habasch * Mircea Dan Duta * Naida Mujkić * Swagat Das

The Lapita

The Poetry Posse 2018

Gail Weston Shazor * Nizar Sartawi * Hülya N. Yılmaz
Jackie Davis Allen * Caroline 'Ceri' Nazareno
Alicja Maria Kuberska * Teresa E. Gallion
Kimberly Burnham * Shareef Abdur – Rasheed
Ashok K. Bhargava* Elizabeth Castillo * Swapna Behaera
Tezmin Ition Tsai * William S. Peters, Sr.

Now Available

www.innerchildpress.com/the-year-of-the-poet

The Year of the Poet V
September 2018

The Aztecs & Incas

Featured Poets
Jyolsda Danitawardo Freedom
Liza Saqiri
Maciej Husseini Abdel Glien
Lily Swarn

The Poetry Posse 2018

Gail Weston Shazor * Nizar Sartawi * Hülya N. Yılmaz
Jackie Davis Allen * Caroline 'Ceri' Nazareno
Alicja Maria Kubenska * Teresa E. Gallion
Kimberly Burnham * Shareef Abdur – Rasheed
Ashok K. Bhargava * Elizabeth Castillo * Swapna Behera
Teemin Ition Tsai * William S. Peters, Sr.

The Year of the Poet V
October 2018

Featured Poets
Alicia Minjarez * Lonnoice Weeks-Badley
Lopamudra Mishra * Abdelwahed Souayah

Bengali

The Poetry Posse 2018

Gail Weston Shazor * Nizar Sartawi * Hülya N. Yılmaz
Jackie Davis Allen * Caroline 'Ceri' Nazareno
Alicja Maria Kubenska * Teresa E. Gallion
Kimberly Burnham * Shareef Abdur – Rasheed
Ashok K. Bhargava * Elizabeth Castillo * Swapna Behera
Teemin Ition Tsai * William S. Peters, Sr.

The Year of the Poet V
November 2018

Featured Poets
Michelle Joan Barulich * Monsif Beroual
Krystyna Konecka * Nassira Nezzar

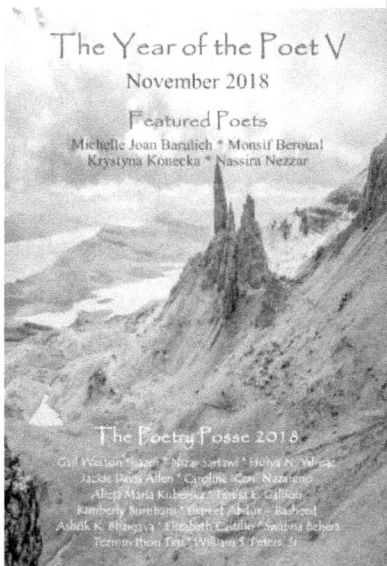

The Poetry Posse 2018

Gail Weston Shazor * Nizar Sartawi * Hülya N. Yılmaz
Jackie Davis Allen * Caroline 'Ceri' Nazareno
Alicja Maria Kubenska * Teresa E. Gallion
Kimberly Burnham * Shareef Abdur – Rasheed
Ashok K. Bhargava * Elizabeth Castillo * Swapna Behera
Teemin Ition Tsai * William S. Peters, Sr.

The Year of the Poet V
December 2018

Featured Poets
Rose Terranova Cirigliano
Joanna Kalinowska
Sokolović Emir
Dr. T. Ashok Chakravarthy

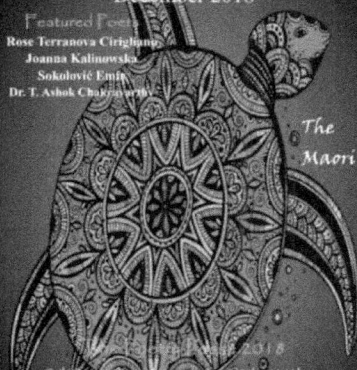

The Maori

The Poetry Posse 2018

Gail Weston Shazor * Nizar Sartawi * Hülya N. Yılmaz
Jackie Davis Allen * Caroline 'Ceri' Nazareno
Alicja Maria Kubenska * Teresa E. Gallion
Kimberly Burnham * Shareef Abdur – Rasheed
Ashok K. Bhargava * Elizabeth Castillo * Swapna Behera
Teemin Ition Tsai * William S. Peters, Sr.

Now Available

www.innerchildpress.com/the-year-of-the-poet

The Year of the Poet VI
January 2019

Indigenous North Americans

Featured Poets

Houda Elfchtali
Anthony Briscoe
Iram Fatima 'Ashi'
Dr. K. K. Mathew

Dream Catcher

The Poetry Posse 2019

Gail Weston Shazor * Joe Paire * Hülya N. Yılmaz
Jackie Davis Allen * Caroline Cen Nazareno
Alicja Maria Kuberska * Teresa E. Gallion
Kimberly Burnham * Shareef Abdur – Rasheed
Ashok K. Bhargava * Elizabeth Castillo * Swapna Behera
Tezmin Ition Tsai * William S. Peters, Sr.

The Year of the Poet VI
February 2019

Featured Poets
Marek Lukaszewicz * Bharati Nayak
Aida G. Roque * Jean-Jacques Fournier

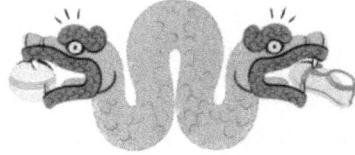

Meso-America

The Poetry Posse 2019

Gail Weston Shazor * Albert Carrasco * Hülya N. Yılmaz
Jackie Davis Allen * Caroline Nazareno * Eliza Segiet
Alicja Maria Kuberska * Teresa E. Gallion * Joe Paire
Kimberly Burnham * Shareef Abdur – Rasheed
Ashok K. Bhargava * Elizabeth Castillo * Swapna Behera
Tezmin Ition Tsai * William S. Peters, Sr.

The Year of the Poet VI
March 2019

Featured Poets
Epesa Mabmié * Sylwia K. Malinowska
Shurouk Hammood * Anwer Ghani

The Caribbean

The Poetry Posse 2019

Gail Weston Shazor * Albert Carrasco * Hülya N. Yılmaz
Jackie Davis Allen * Caroline Nazareno * Eliza Segiet
Alicja Maria Kuberska * Teresa E. Gallion * Joe Paire
Kimberly Burnham * Shareef Abdur – Rasheed
Ashok K. Bhargava * Elizabeth Castillo * Swapna Behera
Tezmin Ition Tsai * William S. Peters, Sr.

The Year of the Poet VI
April 2019

Featured Poets
DL Davis * Michelle Joan Barulich
Lulëzim Haziri * Faleeha Hassan

Central & West Africa

The Poetry Posse 2019

Gail Weston Shazor * Albert Carrasco * Hülya N. Yılmaz
Jackie Davis Allen * Caroline Nazareno * Eliza Segiet
Alicja Maria Kuberska * Teresa E. Gallion * Joe Paire
Kimberly Burnham * Shareef Abdur – Rasheed
Ashok K. Bhargava * Elizabeth Castillo * Swapna Behera
Tezmin Ition Tsai * William S. Peters, Sr.

Now Available

www.innerchildpress.com/the-year-of-the-poet

The Year of the Poet VI
May 2019
Featured Poets
Emad Al-Haydary * Hussein Nasser Jabr
Wahab Sheriff * Abdul Razzaq Al Ameeri

Asia Southeast Asia and Maritime Asia

The Poetry Posse 2019

Gail Weston Shazor * Albert Carrasco * Hülya N. Yilmaz
Jackie Davis Allen * Caroline Nazareno * Eliza Segiet
Alicja Maria Kuberska * Teresa E. Gallion * Joe Paire
Kimberly Burnham * Shareef Abdur – Rasheed
Ashok K. Bhargava * Elizabeth Castillo * Swapna Behera
Tezmin Ition Tsai * William S. Peters, Sr.

The Year of the Poet VI
June 2019
Featured Poets
Kate Gaudi Powiekszone * Sahaj Sabharwal
Iwu Jeff * Mohamed Abdel Aziz Shneis

Arctic Circumpolar

The Poetry Posse 2019

Gail Weston Shazor * Albert Carrasco * Hülya N. Yilmaz
Jackie Davis Allen * Caroline Nazareno * Eliza Segiet
Alicja Maria Kuberska * Teresa E. Gallion * Joe Paire
Kimberly Burnham * Shareef Abdur – Rasheed
Ashok K. Bhargava * Elizabeth Castillo * Swapna Behera
Tezmin Ition Tsai * William S. Peters, Sr.

The Year of the Poet VI
Featured Poets
Saadeddin Shahin - Andy Scott
Fahreddin Shehu - Alok Kumar Rai

The Horn of Africa

Ethiopia   Djibouti
Somalia   Eritrea

The Poetry Posse 2019

Gail Weston Shazor * Albert Carrasco * Hülya N. Yilmaz
Jackie Davis Allen * Caroline Nazareno * Eliza Segiet
Alicja Maria Kuberska * Teresa E. Gallion * Joe Paire
Kimberly Burnham * Shareef Abdur – Rasheed
Ashok K. Bhargava * Elizabeth Castillo * Swapna Behera
Tezmin Ition Tsai * William S. Peters, Sr.

The Year of the Poet VI
August 2019
Featured Poets
Shola Balogun * Bharati Nayak
Monalisa Dash Dwibedy * Mbizo Chirasha

Coexist

Southwest Asia

The Poetry Posse 2019

Gail Weston Shazor * Albert Carrasco * Hülya N. Yilmaz
Jackie Davis Allen * Caroline Nazareno * Eliza Segiet
Alicja Maria Kuberska * Teresa E. Gallion * Joe Paire
Kimberly Burnham * Shareef Abdur – Rasheed
Ashok K. Bhargava * Elizabeth Castillo * Swapna Behera
Tezmin Ition Tsai * William S. Peters, Sr.

Now Available

www.innerchildpress.com/the-year-of-the-poet

The Year of the Poet VI
September 2019

Featured Poets

Elena Liliana Popescu * Gobinda Biswas
Iram Fatima 'Ashi' * Joseph S. Spence, Sr

The Caucasus

The Poetry Posse 2019

Gail Weston Shazor * Albert Carrasco * Hülya N. Yilmaz
Jackie Davis Allen * Caroline Nazareno * Eliza Segiet
Alicja Maria Kuberska * Teresa E. Gallion * Joe Paire
Kimberly Burnham * Shareef Abdur – Rasheed
Ashok K. Bhargava * Elizabeth Castillo * Swapna Behera
Tezmin Ition Tsai * William S. Peters, Sr.

The Year of the Poet VI
October 2019

Featured Poets

Ngozi Olivia Osuoha * Denisa Kondič
Pankhuri Sinha * Christena AV Williams

The Nile Valley

The Poetry Posse 2019

Gail Weston Shazor * Albert Carrasco * Hülya N. Yilmaz
Jackie Davis Allen * Caroline Nazareno * Eliza Segiet
Alicja Maria Kuberska * Teresa E. Gallion * Joe Paire
Kimberly Burnham * Shareef Abdur – Rasheed
Ashok K. Bhargava * Elizabeth Castillo * Swapna Behera
Tezmin Ition Tsai * William S. Peters, Sr.

The Year of the Poet VI
November 2019

Featured Poets

Rozalia Aleksandrova * Orbindu Gangh
Smruti Ranjan Mohanty * Sofia Sklrida

Northern Asia

The Poetry Posse 2019

Gail Weston Shazor * Albert Carrasco * Hülya N. Yilmaz
Jackie Davis Allen * Caroline Nazareno * Eliza Segiet
Alicja Maria Kuberska * Teresa E. Gallion * Joe Paire
Kimberly Burnham * Shareef Abdur – Rasheed
Ashok K. Bhargava * Elizabeth Castillo * Swapna Behera
Tezmin Ition Tsai * William S. Peters, Sr.

The Year of the Poet VI
December 2019

Featured Poets

Rabson Kurniri Kurensis * Sarani Paul
Jhuma Nayak * Kapardeli Eftichia

Oceania

The Poetry Posse 2019

Gail Weston Shazor * Albert Carrasco * Hülya N. Yilmaz
Jackie Davis Allen * Caroline Nazareno * Eliza Segiet
Alicja Maria Kuberska * Teresa E. Gallion * Joe Paire
Kimberly Burnham * Shareef Abdur – Rasheed
Ashok K. Bhargava * Elizabeth Castillo * Swapna Behera
Tezmin Ition Tsai * William S. Peters, Sr.

Now Available

www.innerchildpress.com/the-year-of-the-poet

The Year of the Poet VII
January 2020
Featured Poets
B S Tyagi * Ashok Chakravarthy Tholana
Andy Scott * Anwer Ghani

1901 Jean Henry Dunant and Frédéric Passy

The Year of Peace
Celebrating past Nobel Peace Prize Recipients

The Poetry Posse 2020
Gail Weston Shazor * Albert Carasco * Hülya N. Yılmaz
Jackie Davis Allen * Caroline Nazareno * Eliza Segiet
Alicja Maria Kuberska * Teresa E. Gallion * Joe Paire
Kimberly Burnham * Shareef Abdur – Rasheed
Ashok K. Bhargava * Elizabeth Castillo * Swapna Behera
Tezmin Ition Tsai * William S. Peters, Sr.

The Year of the Poet VII
February 2020
Featured Poets
Jennifer Ades * Martina Reisz Newberry
Ibrahim Honjo * Claudia Piccinno

Henri La Fontaine ~ 1913

The Year of Peace
Celebrating past Nobel Peace Prize Recipients

The Poetry Posse 2020
Gail Weston Shazor * Albert Carasco * Hülya N. Yılmaz
Jackie Davis Allen * Caroline Nazareno * Eliza Segiet
Alicja Maria Kuberska * Teresa E. Gallion * Joe Paire
Kimberly Burnham * Shareef Abdur – Rasheed
Ashok K. Bhargava * Elizabeth Castillo * Swapna Behera
Tezmin Ition Tsai * William S. Peters, Sr.

The Year of the Poet VII
March 2020
Featured Poets
Aziz Mountassir * Krishna Puraisa
Hannie Rouweler * Rozalia Aleksandrova

Aristide Briand ~ 1926 ~ Gustav Stresemann

The Year of Peace
Celebrating past Nobel Peace Prize Recipients

The Poetry Posse 2020
Gail Weston Shazor * Albert Carasco * Hülya N. Yılmaz
Jackie Davis Allen * Caroline Nazareno * Eliza Segiet
Alicja Maria Kuberska * Teresa E. Gallion * Joe Paire
Kimberly Burnham * Shareef Abdur – Rasheed
Ashok K. Bhargava * Elizabeth Castillo * Swapna Behera
Tezmin Ition Tsai * William S. Peters, Sr.

The Year of the Poet VII
April 2020
Featured Poets
Rohini Behera * Mircea Dan Duta
Monalisa Dash Dwibedy * NilavroNill Shoovro

Carlos Saavedra Lamas ~ 1936

The Year of Peace
Celebrating past Nobel Peace Prize Recipients

The Poetry Posse 2020
Gail Weston Shazor * Albert Carasco * Hülya N. Yılmaz
Jackie Davis Allen * Caroline Nazareno * Eliza Segiet
Alicja Maria Kuberska * Teresa E. Gallion * Joe Paire
Kimberly Burnham * Shareef Abdur – Rasheed
Ashok K. Bhargava * Elizabeth Castillo * Swapna Behera
Tezmin Ition Tsai * William S. Peters, Sr.

Now Available

www.innerchildpress.com/the-year-of-the-poet

The Year of the Poet VII
May 2020

Featured Poets

Alok Kumar Ray * Eden S. Trinidad
Franco Barbato * Izabela Zubko

Ralph Bunche ~ 1950

The Year of Peace
Celebrating past Nobel Peace Prize Recipients

The Poetry Posse 2020

Gail Weston Shazor * Albert Carasco * Hülya N. Yilmaz
Jackie Davis Allen * Caroline Nazareno * Eliza Segiet
Alicja Maria Kubenska * Teresa E. Gallion * Joe Paire
Kimberly Burnham * Shareef Abdur – Rasheed
Ashok K. Bhargava * Elizabeth Castillo * Swapna Behera
Tezmin Ition Tsai * William S. Peters, Sr.

The Year of the Poet VII
June 2020

Featured Poets

Ellichia Kapardeli * Metin Cengiz
Hussein Habasch * Kosh K Mathew

Albert John Lutuli ~ 1960

The Year of Peace
Celebrating past Nobel Peace Prize Recipients

The Poetry Posse 2020

Gail Weston Shazor * Albert Carasco * Hülya N. Yilmaz
Jackie Davis Allen * Caroline Nazareno * Eliza Segiet
Alicja Maria Kubenska * Teresa E. Gallion * Joe Paire
Kimberly Burnham * Shareef Abdur – Rasheed
Ashok K. Bhargava * Elizabeth Castillo * Swapna Behera
Tezmin Ition Tsai * William S. Peters, Sr.

The Year of the Poet VII
July 2020

Featured Poets

Mykola Martyniuk * Orbindu Ganga
Roula Pollard * Kam Praktisha

Norman Ernest Borlaug ~ 1970

The Year of Peace
Celebrating past Nobel Peace Prize Recipients

The Poetry Posse 2020

Gail Weston Shazor * Albert Carasco * Hülya N. Yilmaz
Jackie Davis Allen * Caroline Nazareno * Eliza Segiet
Alicja Maria Kubenska * Teresa E. Gallion * Joe Paire
Kimberly Burnham * Shareef Abdur – Rasheed
Ashok K. Bhargava * Elizabeth Castillo * Swapna Behera
Tezmin Ition Tsai * William S. Peters, Sr.

The Year of the Poet VII
August 2020

Featured Poets

Dr Pragya Suman * Chinh Nguyen
Srinivas Vasudev * Ugwu Leonard Ifeanyi, Jr.

Adolfo Pérez Esquivel ~ 1980

The Year of Peace
Celebrating past Nobel Peace Prize Recipients

The Poetry Posse 2020

Gail Weston Shazor * Albert Carasco * Hülya N. Yilmaz
Jackie Davis Allen * Caroline Nazareno * Eliza Segiet
Alicja Maria Kubenska * Teresa E. Gallion * Joe Paire
Kimberly Burnham * Shareef Abdur – Rasheed
Ashok K. Bhargava * Elizabeth Castillo * Swapna Behera
Tezmin Ition Tsai * William S. Peters, Sr.

Now Available

www.innerchildpress.com/the-year-of-the-poet

and there is much, much more !

visit . . .

www.innerchildpress.com/antho
logies-sales-special.php

Also check out our Authors and
all the wonderful Books
Available at :

www.innerchildpress.com/autho
rs-pages

World Healing World Peace
2020

Poets for Humanity

INNER CHILD PRESS

WORLD HEALING WORLD PEACE

2018

A Poetry Anthology for Humanity

Now Available

www.worldhealingworldpeacepoetry.com

support

World Healing
World Peace

www.worldhealingworldpeacepoetry.com

216

World Healing ✿ World Peace

Poetry

i am a believer !

World Healing
World Peace
2012, 2014, 2016, 2018, 2020

Now Available

www.worldhealingworldpeacepoetry.com

Inner Child Press International

'building bridges of cultural understanding'

Meet the Board of Directors

www.innerchildpress.com

Inner Child Press International

'building bridges of cultural understanding'

Meet our Cultural Ambassadors

Fahredin Shehu
Director of Cultural

Faleha Hassan
Iraq ~ USA

Elizabeth E. Castillo
Philippines

Antoinette Coleman
Chicago
Midwest USA

Ananda Nepali
Nepal ~ India
Northern India

Kimberly Burnham
Pacific Northwest
USA

Alicja Kuberska
Poland
Eastern Europe

Swapna Behera
India
Southeast Asia

Kolade O. Freedom
Nigeria
West Africa

Monsif Beroual
Morocco
Northern Africa

Ashok K. Bhargava
Canada

Tzemin Ition Tsai
Republic of China
Greater China

Alicia M. Ramirez
Mexico
Central America

Christena AV Williams
Jamaica
Caribbean

Louise Hudon
Eastern Canada

Aziz Mountassir
Morocco
Northern Africa

Shareef Abdur-Rasheed
Southeastern USA

Laure Charazac
France
Western Europe

Muhammad Ikbal Harb
Lebanon
Middle East

**Mohamed Abdel
Aziz Shmeis**
Egypt
Middle East

Hilary Msinga
Kenya
Eastern Africa

Josephus R. Johnson
Liberia

www.innerchildpress.com

This Anthological Publication
is underwritten solely by

Inner Child Press International

Inner Child Press is a Publishing Company Founded and Operated by Writers. Our personal publishing experiences provides us an intimate understanding of the sometimes daunting challenges Writers, New and Seasoned may face in the Business of Publishing and Marketing their Creative "Written Work".

For more Information

Inner Child Press International

www.innerchildpress.com

'building bridges of cultural understanding'

www.innerchildpress.com

202 Wiltree Court, State College, Pennsylvania 16801

~ fini ~

www.ingramcontent.com/pod-product-compliance
Lightning Source LLC
LaVergne TN
LVHW051045080426
835508LV00019B/1713